ASK AUGUSTINE

Is the desire for sex wrong?
Do Moslems believe in the Bible?
Who was the first woman to translate the Bible?
Is reincarnation possible?
What does the Bible say about spiritual mediums?
What is the Messianic Secret?
Were Jesus and Mary married as stated in The DaVinci Code?
... and more

by: Paul A. Tambrino, Ed.D., Ph.D.

xulon
PRESS

Ask Augustine
by Paul A. Tambrino, Ed.D., Ph.D.

Printed in the United States of America

ISBN 1-59781-894-1

www.xulonpress.com

Paul A. Tambio
II Timothy 1:13

ENDORSEMENTS

In his collected columns, Dr. Paul Tambrino shows himself to be a theologian and a churchman to be heard. His thoughtful reflections on a host of contemporary issues apply the transcendent truth of Scripture to the ever-changing issues of our world. He is to be congratulated for making these essays available to all of us who wrestle with the relationship between Christ and Culture.
R. J. Gore Jr., Ph.D.
Dean (former acting President), Erskine Theological Seminary

In this timely volume, Paul Tambrino offers the best of his "Ask Augustine" columns. Paul has the remarkable virtue of being able to summarize and explain, succinctly and clearly, great truths of the Christian Gospel and various contours of theological creeds, beliefs, and divergent opinions of the world religions. I am pleased to endorse such a rich theological feast fit for our age. I think Augustine would approve, too. Bravo!
Prof. Edward N. Martin, Ph.D.
School of Religion, Liberty University, former Academic Vice-President, Trinity Theological Seminary

There are very few scholars who can knowledgeably address a wide range of issues – from biblical theology, to ethics, to systematics, to comparative religions. That is why Dr. Tambrino's "Ask Augustine" columns are a delight to read and ponder. Just as important is Tambrino's obvious respect for the intelligence of his audience. He not only provides well-researched and objective responses to their inquiries but frames the issues raised by each question in ways that encourage further thought and reflection. This collection of "Ask Augustine" columns will provide a valuable resource on important issues in theology and religion.
Lynne Courter Boughton, Ph.D.
University of St. Mary of the Lake/Mundelein Seminary

Tambrino's work is an easily understood, ready resource for some of the most commonly asked questions regarding the Christian faith. This would be a valuable resource for any library and a great tool for sharing Christ with others.
Dr. David Swanson,
Senior Pastor, First Presbyterian Church of Orlando, Florida

As a talk show host, I'm always on the alert for fresh minds and clarity of thought and I always latch onto the latest installment of Paul's "Ask Augustine" as an example of both.
Jan Mickelson
WHO/WMT Radio, Des Moines

I have always been grateful to Augustine and the other gifted leaders of the Church to lead us back to the Word of God in our search for truth and the living of our lives. Augustine and Tambrino had always dedicated their gifts to the Glory of the Risen and Ascended Lord. As a fellow Yankee fan I

also appreciate the humorous way in which he included a question or two about the greatest team in baseball.
Mark E. Salmon, D.Min.
Grace Presbyterian Church, Corpus Christi, Texas

Dr. Tambrino has compiled a helpful tool for interested laypersons, Seminarians and Pastors seeking accessible and reliable information on a broad variety of Biblical and theological questions and answers. "Ask Augustine" will prove a useful resource for every Christian's library.
Pastor Rebecca M.M. Heber (E.L.C.A.), Zellwood, Florida

It is refreshing to find a retired college president who can debunk biblical and religious false teachings and legends and bridge the gap between "so-called" modern questions with solid theological reflection. Thank you, Dr. Tambrino.
Rev. Phil Arnold
Pastor, First Reformed Church (RCA), Alexander, Iowa

"Ask Augustine" is a tremendous resource from a man who deeply loves God and Christ's Church, who understands culture and has the experience, intellect and pastor's heart to bring the light of truth into dark places.
Jeff Jakes
Pastor, Orangewood Presbyterian Church, Maitland, Florida

Dr. Paul Tambrino has devoted his life to education and teaching. Ask Augustine extends that teaching to us readers with helpful insights to expand our understanding of the Bible and Christian theology. It will be a real addition to the bookshelf of any serious student of Scripture.
Dr. Paige M. McRight
Executive Presbyter, Central Florida Presbytery

Critical (in the best sense of the word) theological thinking becomes a more precious commodity in the world and in the church with each passing day. Scholarly reflection on today's issues that is put in words that the everyday Christian can glean from is an even more precious commodity. Therefore, when you find it, you treasure it. For years, Paul Tambrino's writings have been a treasure to me and now you have the same opportunity to be challenged in your faith and moved to Christian action through this new book.

Rev. Jim Koopman
Regional Minister, Reformed Church in America, Synod of the Heartland

Book Summary

For the past several years the author has been writing a newspaper column to supply brief, yet adequate and reliable answers to a great number of popular questions about biblical and theological issues. The process of writing this book included selecting those questions that were the most frequently asked and particularly those that have been persistently asked through the years. It is amazing how many things are attributed to the Bible that are not in it. Homespun Scripture and folklore result from making the Bible say things it does not say and distorting things that it does say.

Ask Augustine is much more than a simple question and answer book. Questions are used to challenge the reader's attention and to present information in the most effective manner. The book is a series of short essays ranging in length from a sentence or two to several pages. It is not a biblical or theological commentary, concordance, dictionary, or encyclopedia, but embraces some of the characteristics of them all.

The author makes no claim that he has avoided the subjective element, which colors all our thinking about the Bible and theological doctrines. Inevitably one's own predilections and biases get in the way. Nevertheless, he has tried to be as objective, impartial, clear and as brief as possible.

The author would like to give the source and authority for every statement made in this book, but so many sources and authorities have been consulted and so many persons have helped, that it is impracticable to even try to list them. Because most of the questions in this book defy classification, there is no general scheme of arrangement unless random order may be regarded as such. It is believed the sudden change from topic to topic presents information in the most direct and interesting manner.

CONTENTS

Why is this book titled, "Ask Augustine" and who was Augustine?

"Ask Augustine" is titled after Aurelius Augustinus, one of the greatest theologians of Western Christianity. Indeed, his name is seldom uttered with the appellation "Saint." He was born 13 November 354 in North Africa, about 45 miles south of the Mediterranean, in the town of Tagaste in Numidia (now Souk-Ahras in Algeria), near ancient Carthage (modern Tunis). His mother, Monica, was a Christian and his father, Patricius, was a pagan for many years but reportedly became a Christian and was baptized just before his death in 370. Augustine had and older brother, Navigius and a sister whose name was never mentioned.

His mother was a devout Christian who prayed for her son without fail, but he was more interested in the attractions of sex, fame, and pride in his own cleverness. By his own confession, Augustine was a wild and lawless youth. He stole simply for the pleasure of stealing and excelled at lying. At 18 he went to Carthage where he became chief in the school of rhetoric. After a moderate amount of running around as a teen-ager, he took a mistress, with whom he lived for 15 years. She bore him his only son, Adeodatus, which literally means "gift of God".

He became engrossed in the theater and the imaginary joys and sorrows of its actors but was set free from this fantasy when he read a treatise by Cicero that opened his eyes to the delights of philosophy. He was a brilliant student, with an eager intellectual curiosity, but he never mastered Greek. He tells us that his first Greek teacher was a brutal man who constantly beat his students, and Augustine rebelled and vowed never to learn Greek. By the time he realized that he really needed to know Greek, it was too late; and although he acquired a smattering of the language, he was never really at home in it. However, his mastery of Latin was another matter. He became an expert both in the eloquent use of the language and in the use of clever arguments to make his points.

Augustine was enamored with Manicheanism for nine years. Manicheanism is named for Mani, a Persian who had preached kind of synthesis of Christianity with Zoroastrianism, the dominant religion of Persia. Zoroaster had taught a radical form of metaphysical dualism. The Manicheans believed there were two eternal and equally opposing forces of good and evil locked in endless combat.

Augustine went to Rome hoping to teach rhetoric, but when no openings became available he traveled to Milan and resumed his teaching career. While in Milan, Augustine came under the influence of its intelligent and articulate bishop, Ambrose. For the first time, Augustine saw Christianity as a religion fit for a philosopher. However, if there was a decisive human factor in his ultimate conversion, it was his mother Monica and her undying intercession.

The major obstacle in Augustine's life was not intellectual but moral. One of his prayers was, "Grant me chastity and continence, but not yet!" There is some disagreement about the extent of his sexual activity. It has been argued that he was sexually faithful to his mistress and after he ended the relationship he took a "stopgap" mistress to whom he was also faithful to tide him over until the marriage. Those who make this argument note that it is characteristic that after he ended the 15 year relationship with his first mistress he did not resort to promiscuity, but to another sole concubine.

While in Milan, Augustine became a neo-Platonist. Plato, as interpreted by Plotinus, taught that only God is fully real, and that all other things are degenerations in varying degrees from the One; that things are progressively less good, less spiritual, and less real as one goes rung by rung down the cosmic ladder. By contemplating spiritual realities, directing one's attention first to one's own mind and then moving up the ladder rung by one to the contemplation of God, one acquires true wisdom, true self-fulfillment, true spirituality, and union with God, or the One. Augustine undertook this approach, and believed that he had an experience of the presence of God. But found this only made him more aware of the great gulf between what he was and what he ought to be.

Meanwhile, he continued to hear the preaching and teaching of Bishop Ambrose. Finally, partly because Ambrose had answers for his questions, partly because he admired Ambrose personally, but chiefly because God touched his heart, he was converted to Christianity in 386. Ambrose baptized him on Easter in 387. About 12 years later he wrote an account of his life up to a time shortly after his conversion. This book called the *Confessions*, is an outpouring of penitence and thanksgiving.

Notwithstanding his struggles, the Lord had graciously sought him out. He wrote that while he was praying these words, "How long, how long? Tomorrow and tomorrow? Why not now? Why is there not this hour an end to my uncleanness?" It was then he heard what seemed to be a child's voice coming from a neighboring house, saying over and over, "Tolle, lege; tolle, lege." (Take up and read; pick up and read). Since he could not think of any reason why a child would be saying that, he took it as an omen, and picked up a copy of Paul's Epistle to the Romans. As he opened it, his eye fell on the end of the thirteenth chapter where he read these words, "Let us walk honestly, as in the day; not in rioting and drunkenness, not in chambering and wantonness, not in strife and envying. But put ye on the Lord Jesus Christ, and make not provision for the flesh, to fulfill the lusts thereof." As he read, he experienced this as God speaking directly to him, convicting him of his past sins, and offering him forgiveness; calling him to amend his life, and promising him the grace and power to do it. He burst into tears, and surrendered. After his conversion, Augustine went back to his native Africa where he was ordained a priest in 391 and consecrated bishop of Hippo in 396. He was a diligent shepherd of his flock, but he also found time to write extensively.

His work greatly influenced Luther and Calvin, to the point where for a while Roman Catholics were wary of quoting him lest they be suspected of Protestant tendencies. In addition to his *Confessions*, he also wrote, *De Civitate Dei* ("The City of God") and *De Trinitate* ("On the Trinity"). One of my favorite quotes from Augustine basically sums up his conversion experience, "God chooses us, not because we believe, but that we may believe."

If the Christian era begins with the birth of Jesus, why doesn't our calendar year start on December 25?

The Christian era theoretically begins with the birth of Jesus Christ, but the calendar year begins January 1 instead of December 25, the traditional birthday of Jesus. This anomalous situation is due to the fact that the Christian era was not calculated until the sixth century and was not generally accepted in Christendom until about the year 1000. Consequently the beginning of the era was projected into the past.

The Romans reckoned time from the legendary date of the founding of Rome. The starting point in Roman chronology was *Anno Urbis Conditae* (AU.C.), which literally means "in the year of the founded city." About 532 A.D., after Christianity had become dominant in the old Roman Empire, a learned monk of Rome named Dionysius Exiguus worked out a Christian system of chronology to take the place of the then prevalent pagan system. He concluded that Jesus was born December 25, 753 A.U.C.

During the first centuries there was little uniformity in the date observed as the nativity. The first *Christ-mass* was celebrated on December 25 in Rome about 350 A.D., but this was regarded as a legendary date as Christmas was observed on different days throughout Christendom. Dionysius should have begun the new era with December 25, but he decided to begin it with January 1 because he wanted to leave the Roman year and months intact and did not want to upset the established order. Accordingly he began the Christian era with the first day in 754 A.U.C. His new system did not completely supplant the old system in the Western world until about 1000A.D. Emperor Charles III of Germany was the first sovereign to adopt the new system and in 879 A.D. he adopted *Anno Domini*, "in the year of the Lord.

Modern scholars believe Dionysius was off several years in fixing the birth date of Jesus Christ and consequently we have the anomalous situation of Christ having been born at least four of five years before the beginning of the era that bears his name. After the Christian calendar and era became firmly established with December 25 as Christmas, it was impractical to change it and upset the entire system.

As a matter of fact, the entire Christian world is not yet in agreement even on the traditional day of the birth of Jesus. While Roman Catholics and Protestants generally observe Christmas on December 25, Orthodox Greek Catholics observe it on January 6 and the Armenian Church on January 19.

The epoch beginning with the birth of Jesus is also called the "common era", particularly by orthodox Jews, who are compelled to recognize it for practical purposes but who object to it as the Christian era on the ground that such notice might be interpreted as a recognition of its founder. Strict Jews who use the Christian date seldom add the letters A.D.

The Jewish calendar reckons time from the year 3761 B.C, the traditional date of creation of man. This Jewish calendar, which assumed its present form in the fourth century A.D. in the time of Hillel II, is based on the motions of both the sun and the moon and in consequence the Jewish New Year and other holidays do not fall on the same date each year according to the Gregorian calendar. Although Christmas is a fixed date in the Christian calendar, Easter and certain other church days are variable dates and are determined somewhat after the manner of the Jewish calendar.

On what day was Christ born?

While no one knows precisely when Jesus was born, over the years many have objected to celebrating the His birth on December 25 as they link that date with the pagan Roman celebration of Saturnalia. However, it is far more likely that the date was chosen because of the Jewish festival of Hanukkah.

In 168 B.C. Antiochus Epiphanes began a campaign of atrocities against the Jews, killing thousands of them and defiling the sacred alter in the temple. The temple was looted and further defiled when a statue of Zeus Olympus was erected in the Holy of Holies. These acts of degradation were met by rebellion by a priest named Mattathias and his five sons who would later take on the family name of Maccabee. After three years of fighting the Maccabean army drove the infidels out of the land. One of the Maccabees' first actions was to cleanse and rededicate the temple, which marked the beginning of Hanukkah (to dedicate). The dedication was on the 25th. of Chislev, or December 25 and is referred to in John 10:22 as "the feast of dedication."

Years later a tradition arose that during the temple cleansing, they found a one-day supply of oil for the Menorah, or seven-branched candelabrum. It would take days to ceremonially prepare more oil and a miracle is supposed to have occurred when the one-day supply of oil lasted for eight. That is why there are eight candles lit during Hanukkah.

After Jesus' death, burial and resurrection, Hebrew Christians began to associate the light, Jesus, the temple and Hanukkah. This is why the center branch of the menorah stands taller than the other eight. It is called the *shamash*, or "servant" candle and was the early Christians' way of illustrating John 1:9, "This was the true light that gives light to every man who comes into the world." Therefore, when the church needed a date to designate the time for observing Christ's birth, it could find no better one than December 25.

Many parts of the world celebrate a holiday on September 29 called Michaelmaus Day. It means "Michael Sent" just as Christmas means "Christ Sent." Some biblical scholars believe that it was Michael who was sent with the heavenly host to proclaim the birth to the shepherds (Luke 2:9-15). September 29 corresponds with the 15th. of Tishri on the Hebrew calendar, the beginning of the Feat of Tabernacles. This festive holiday commemorates God's provision in the wilderness, when the children of Israel dwelt in tents or tabernacles. The New Testament tells us, "The Word became flesh and lived (tabernacled) for a while among us."

September 29 was the logical time for a Roman census as the crops were in and the people were at liberty. The Bible tells us "there were shepherds living out in the fields nearby, keeping watch over their flocks at night" (Luke 2:8). This took place only in the summer and the fall; by October or November the flocks were gathered in because of the cold. Other scholars claim that the Roman census almost always occurred between August and October giving further evidence that the actual birth of Christ may have occurred during the Feast of Tabernacles.

If the birth of Christ occurred on September 29, given a human gestation period of 278 days, ironically the supernatural conception by the Holy Spirit in the womb of Mary would be December 25. Nevertheless, the real issue for Christians is not whether Christ was born on December 25 or September 29 but rather when He is born in them.

What is Hanukkah?

Hanukkah is the Hebrew word for dedication and is pronounced CHA-nu-ka. Although it is a Jewish holiday, the only mention of it in the Bible is found in John 10:22-23 in the New Testament, "Now it was the Feast of Dedication in Jerusalem, and it was winter. And Jesus walked in the temple, in Solomon's porch." However, the story is found in First and Second Maccabees, books which are not recognized as part of the canon of Scripture by either the Jews or the Protestants, but which are considered canonical by Roman Catholics. The Jewish historian, Josephus mentions the term Hanukkah in his history of Hanukkah. He explains, "The festival acquired this name because the right to serve God came to the people unexpectedly, as a light."

The holiday lasts for eight days. When kindling the lights, two benedictions are recited, one is a blessing on the lights and the other for the miracle. On the first night the blessing for the season is added and short prayer follows the kindling of the light. A summary of the event is recited in prayer and in the Grace after Meals. The entire *Hallel* (Praise of God), Psalms 113-118, is said on each of the eight days. The reading of the law is from the portion of the Torah, which describes the sacrifices brought by the princes at the dedication of the sanctuary, and the kindling of the candelabrum (Num. 7:1–8:4).

The story of Hanukkah is the age-old story of Jewish struggle for survival in a hostile gentile world. During the second century the Greek King Antiochus Epiphanes ruled Israel. The Greeks at that time worshipped many gods and goddesses. The Jewish people were divided into two groups, the Hellenists who adopted the Greek way and the Hasidim who adhered to the laws of the Torah and refused to pay homage to the Greek gods.

King Antiochus was intolerant of the Jewish ways. He converted the Holy Temple in Jerusalem into a temple of Zeus. He placed a statue of himself in the temple, declared himself to be a god and held drunken orgies in the rooms of the temple. A family (the Mattathias family) of righteous Jews, who lived in the village of Modin, revolted. Judah Maccabee, the son of Mattathias, led the revolt, which lasted almost three years. When the Maccabees reclaimed Jerusalem they found the Temple in ruins. They began to restore the Temple and on the 25th. day of Kislev the Temple was rededicated. A small amount of pure oil was found that was enough to keep the Temple menorah burning for one day, yet it miraculously lasted for eight days. Hence, the origin of the eight day celebration of Hanukkah and the eight branch menorah that is lit on each of the eight nights. A ninth candle, the shammash (servant) is used to light the others.

Was Jesus descended from David?

The New Testament clearly represents Jesus as a descendant of David. Prophecy foretold that the Messiah would be a descendant of David and "the Son of David" had been the accepted title of the Messiah among the Jews for generations. In the Gospels Jesus is frequently referred to as the Son of David.

Matthew 1:18 says, "Now the birth of Jesus was as follows: After His mother Mary was betrothed to Joseph, before they came together, she was found with child of the

Holy Spirit." Luke 3:23 refers to Jesus as, "being (as was supposed) the son of Joseph." Since Joseph was not the blood father of Jesus, the inference is that Mary as well as Joseph was of the house and lineage of David, although the New Testament nowhere specifically says that about Mary. Luke 1:27 says the angel Gabriel was sent "to a virgin betrothed to a man whose name was Joseph, of the house of David. The virgin's name was Mary."

But in Romans 1:3 Paul says Jesus "was born of the seed of David according to the flesh." According to Luke 1:32, Gabriel told Mary that the Lord would give her Son "the throne of His father David," and in Revelation 22:16 Jesus refers to Himself as "the Root and the Offspring of David."

The Davidic descent of Mary has been assumed since Apostolic (early church) times and the passages quoted indicate that Jesus was descended from David through His mother. Among the Israelites it was customary to trace descent only through the male line.

The genealogies in both Matthew and Luke trace the descent of Joseph from David. Although neither literally includes the genealogy of Mary, the genealogies in the two Gospels are considerably different. Matthew traces the genealogy all the way back to Adam while Luke traces it back only to Abraham. Some of the names and the order in the two genealogies differ as well. Some theologians have suggested that Matthew has Joseph's line and Luke Mary's, but Luke specifically starts with "Joseph." It may be that Matthew is not giving direct ancestors but those who would have been legally in line for the throne of David. In any event, both evangelists clearly emphasize that Jesus was of Davidic descent.

Whose birthday do we celebrate on December 25?

At first glance, I thought this was a facetious question; but within several hours a series of events led me to conclude otherwise.

Shortly after receiving this question I attended a meeting at the clubhouse in our housing development and noticed that it had been decorated with brightly colored lights. A quick glance about the room made me proud that we had honored the diversity of our residents. A "Happy Kwanzaa" sign was displayed prominently by the entryway; two "Happy Hanukah" signs appeared on either side of the door and a beautiful white and blue tapestry depicting the Star of David with the word "Shalom" hung on the rear wall. Several pictures of a dreidel were scattered on the four walls along with snowmen and a Santa Claus here and there. The tree and wreath that were there really said little if anything about meaning of Christmas. Nowhere was there any sign saying "Merry Christmas" much less any depiction of the first Christmas.

When I asked a member of the decorating committee about the absence of a "Merry Christmas" sign, she stated that her committee had the same concern but such a sign was nowhere to be found. Nonsense, I thought. I'll purchase one and hang it myself.

My wife and I spent the entire afternoon looking through major department stores, leading discount stores, supermarkets and well known pharmacies with no success in finding a sign. Now, I'm not one who believes that there is some sinister plot to eliminate Christmas, but I can tell you that in our extensive search we found lots of signs and things that read "happy holidays," and "season's greetings," but none that read "Merry Christmas." One well-known pharmacy had sweatshirts that read. "Dear Santa: <u>I want it all</u>! How sad I thought; we have forgotten that in the true meaning of Christmas we have it all!!! It is sheer ignorance and nonsense to pretend that Christmas (the birthday of Christ) is not the epicenter of the season.

Was Jesus born in a stable?

A local tradition dating back at least to the second century places the manger and nativity in a grotto or cave near Bethlehem. In 165 A.D. St. Justin wrote, "Having failed to find any lodging in the town, Joseph sought shelter in a neighboring cavern of Bethlehem." About a half-century later the celebrated ecclesiastical writer Origen declared that, "at Bethlehem is shown the grotto where he first saw the light." The shepherds and their flocks, it is supposed, used this grotto, as a shelter. St. Helena, mother of Constantine the Great, identified a grotto near Bethlehem as the birthplace of Jesus and had it converted into a chapel. Later a basilica was erected over the grotto.

Matthew 2:11 only tells us that the wise men (who probably arrived sometime after the Birth of Jesus) came into the house and when they saw the young child they fell down and worshipped Him. Manger is used three times by Luke in chapter two, verses seven, twelve and sixteen. A manger, properly speaking, is a trough or box from which domestic animals eat. The Greek word rendered manger in the passages from Luke is derived from a verb meaning to eat and literally means feeding place. Some suppose that the manger in which Mary laid the child was in the court of an inn or caravansary. The typical Near Eastern Inn of that day consisted of a rude, unfurnished shelter surrounding a court in which the camels, horses, and other beasts of burden were picketed.

Again, for Christians, the essential question is not whether Jesus was born in a manger in a stable, but whether He has been born in them.

Were the shepherds and wise men the same persons?

Some authorities incline toward the opinion that the shepherds' who visited the newborn Jesus were the same persons as the wise men who came from the East. Only the Gospel of Mathew records the story of the wise men, and only the Gospel of Luke records the story of the shepherds. The Gospels of Mark and John refer to neither the shepherds nor the wise men, or for that matter, any of the *physical* events surrounding Jesus' birth.

The passage in Luke (chapter 2 verses 8 through 20), which provides the only biblical information we have about the shepherds who visited the newborn Jesus, has many points in common with the story of the wise men related in Mathew (chapter 2 verses 1 through 12). Although some authorities regard the two as merely different versions of the same event, there is not sufficient evidence to establish that these shepherds and the wise men were the same persons. The conventional opinion is that they were not the same.

Who were the Three Wise Men from the East?

The names number and nationality of the wise men from the East who followed the star of the newborn Jesus to Jerusalem and Bethlehem are not given in the Bible. This beautiful story is told in Matthew 2:1-12, and that is all the information there is in the Bible about the wise men.

Early traditional writers fixed their number at three, probably because three gifts are mentioned. A legend, apparently dating from the second or third century, refers to them as kings. Later legends give them names: Gasper (white), Melchior (light) and Balthasar (lord of the treasury house).

Many Bible scholars suppose the three wise men to have been Magi, members of the priestly caste in Persia. This opinion is supported by two circumstances: in Palestine *the east* generally refers to Persia; and the religion of the Magi, which was similar to that of Zoroaster, included belief in the advent of a messiah.

The book of travels by Marco Polo 1299 A.D. contains an interesting reference to this subject. Marco Polo wrote of a city in Persia called Saba, in which the three Magi are supposedly buried.

A medieval legend speaks of them as "the three kings of Cologne." According to this legend, Helena, the mother of Constantine the Great, discovered the bones of the Magi in Persia and took them to Constantinople. In 1162 the Emperor Frederick Barbarossa took them from Milan to the Cologne cathedral where the skulls have been exhibited for many centuries.

The names of the three kings were widely used as a charm, and it was believed that those who touched the bones would be healed of all diseases. However, all of this is extra-biblical in nature.

How are the statements in Mary's Magnificat found in Like 1:46-56 related to Jesus' ministry?

The family that Jesus is born into is a peasant family. When He is about one month old the family brings Him to Jerusalem for His dedication and the purification of Mary after giving birth. At this ceremony they give two doves, the offering of a woman who cannot afford a lamb. (Lev. 12:8)

The song of Mary, "The Magnificat," (which means magnify, the opening word in the Latin translation) in Luke 1:46-56 is predictive of Jesus' ministry. This song is patterned after the song of Hannah in I Samuel 2: 1-10. In each case we have a lowly and seemly forgotten and unimportant woman who is given a child against all odds, leading to a song that testifies to the greatness of God and His activity on behalf of the poor and weak who exchange places with the mighty and powerful. God is praised in this song for what He has done, using past tense verbs especially in v 51-53 This can be seen not only as an expression of timeless truth, but also as a statement of confidence that what God has promised can be stated as accomplished fact: He will certainly do it, even if its' full accomplishment awaits the end time.

In this song of Mary we read that He (the God-man Jesus Christ) does great things, His name is holy, He has mercy on those who fear Him, He scatters the proud (especially the Scribes, Pharisees and Sadducees of the day). He pulls the mighty from their thrones, exalts the lowly, and feeds the hungry while the rich go away empty.

What is the significance of the curse on Jechoniah and the Virgin Birth?

Matthew 1:11 included Jechoniah in Jesus' lineage while Luke does not. The critical issue here is the curse on Jechoniah (found in Jeremiah 22:24-30), which precludes him from having any natural descendant upon the throne of David. Thus, Matthew, by giving us the genealogy of Joseph (who was not Jesus' natural father), excludes Jesus as a natural descendant of Jechoniah. If Joseph had been the natural father of Jesus, then the Jesus as Lord would not be able to occupy David's throne and Luke 1:32 and 33 (which states that God gave Jesus the throne of David to reign over the house of Jacob) would contradict the Jechoniah prophecy. But, if Jesus' genealogy through Mary is recorded in Luke, this avoids the curse upon Jechoniah since Jesus' natural descent came only through the "Virgin" Mary.

Many liberal theologians, who do not believe in the predictive prophecy of the Old Testament, argue that the term "virgin" in Isaiah 7:14 should be translated "young maiden" or "young woman." Is this a better translation?

Isaiah 7:14, "Therefore the Lord himself shall give you a sign; Behold, a virgin shall conceive, and bear a son, and shall call his name Immanuel," calls our attention to an important birth and is cited as a Messianic text that also refers to Mary. However, there is often disagreement whether these verses are a literal reference to the Messiah and to His mother Mary. In this passage we are told to look with anticipation to the virgin and her Son who are announced as central figures in this prophecy.

The real questions in this passage are who is the virgin and who is Immanuel? A better reading of the passage should be "the virgin" instead of "a virgin" because the use of the Hebrew definite article in connection with the passage indicates that a definite woman is the mind of the prophet. When the prophet refers to her as "the virgin," it is highly unlikely that he meant to refer to any woman who might bear a child in the next few months. The passage begins by noting that the conception was to be a "sign" to the house of David. The normal conception of a "young married woman" would hardly be considered a "sign"

Those who make the argument for not translating the word in the Hebrew text found in Isaiah 7:14 as "virgin," point out that the word used is the unique and uncommon word *'almah* and had Isaiah meant virgin he would have used the word *bethulah* because that is the more commonly used Hebrew word for virgin. But in spite of its frequent use to specifically denote a virgin, *bethulah* is used in at least one passage (Deuteronomy 22:19) to refer to a young non-virgin woman. Therefore, Isaiah's choice of the rare word *'almah* better signifies virginity than the more common term *bethulah.* While it is true that *'almah* can be translated "young woman," it is never intended in the Hebrew language to deny the legitimacy of a young woman's virginity. In fact it appears six other times in the Old Testament (Genesis 24:43; Exodus 2:8; Psalms 68:25; Proverbs 30:19; and Song of Solomon 1:3, 6:8). A study of each of these contexts reveals that *almah* is used only of one who is a virgin.

Moreover, the Septuagint (a pre-Christian Greek version of the Hebrew Scriptures that dates from the 3rd century B. C.) translated *'almah* by using the Greek word *parthenos*, which always means virgin. Thus, we have a Jewish interpretation of Isaiah 7:14 that is much earlier than when Matthew uses the same word *parthenos* in Matthew 1:23 ("Behold, a virgin shall be with child, and shall bring forth a son, and they shall call his name Emmanuel"), when he refers back to the Isaiah passage.

Immanuel, or Emmanuel, is the symbolic name of the child, meaning "God with us." It is obvious that Matthew regarded this Immanuel to be none other than Jesus Christ Himself. He quoted this prophecy as being fulfilled in the virgin birth (Matthew 1:23) and he considered the birth to be of divine origin, stating that it was "spoken of by the Lord by the prophet" (Matthew 1:22). He therefore recognized that the sign given in Isaiah 7:14 was authored by God and delivered to Ahaz through the prophet. There was no doubt until the rise of modern liberal scholarship that those closest historically to the actual statement found in Isaiah 7:14 by the prophet Isaiah have always taken it to be a prediction of the miraculous virgin birth of the coming Messiah.

What manner of man was Jesus physically?

The Bible gives us no description of the physique of Jesus and there is no known contemporaneous description of Him. Accordingly, we have no means of knowing His height, weight, complexion, color of His eyes, whether He wore a beard or was clean-shaven, His clothing size or anything else about His physical appearance.

Speaking of His childhood, Luke 2:53 says Jesus, "increased in wisdom and stature. In His youth he worked as a carpenter and his public ministry was spent largely in the open air. He fasted forty days in the wilderness, taught multitudes in the mountains and in the valley, sailed on the fishing boats of His followers, and made many long journeys on foot. Every action of His that is recorded in the Gospels indicates that He was a man of strong physique, physical courage and outdoor activity.

The Synoptic Gospels (Matthew, Mark and Luke) tell us that Simon of Cyrene was compelled to bear the cross of Jesus, but this is not conclusive evidence that Jesus was unable to carry the cross. John 19:17 says He "bore His cross," which probably means that He bore it part way to Calvary.

According to tradition, members of the house of David were light complexioned. Since Jesus was a descendant of that family and lineage, artists have generally portrayed Jesus as a blond. But even the earliest extant pictures of Jesus appear to be conventional representations rather than realistic likenesses. A picture of Him in the Roman catacombs, said to date from the second century, represents Him with long, curled hair, short, neatly trimmed beard and mustache, and haven lips. In his "Last Judgment" Michelangelo represented Jesus as beardless.

Are there any extra-biblical accounts of what Jesus looked like?

From time to time reports have been published of the finding of a new description or portrait of Jesus made by a contemporary writer or artist who probably was an eyewitness to the crucifixion, but none of these have proved genuine. One of the most interesting of these is the Lentulus letter. This curious document purports to be a description of Jesus written in the form of a letter to the Roman senate by Publius Lentulus, governor of Judaea during the reign of Tiberius Caesar. It has been quoted as genuine so frequently that it is worth repeating. It reads:

> There hath appeared in these days, a man of great virtue, named Jesus Christ, who is yet living among us, and of the Gentiles is accepted as a Prophet, but his disciples call him the Son of God. He raiseth the dead, and cures all manner of diseases; a man of stature

> somewhat tall and comely, with very reverent countenance, such as beholders both love and fear; his hair the color of chestnut, full ripe, plain to his shoulders. In the midst of his head is a seam or partition of his hair after the manner of the Nazarites; his forehead plain and very delicate; his face without a spot or wrinkle, beautiful with a most lovely red, his nose and mouth so formed that nothing can be reprehended; his beard thickish, in color like his hair, not very long but forked; his look, innocent and mature; his eyes, gray, clear and quick. In reproving he is terrible; in admonishing, courteous, and fair spoken; pleasant in conversation, mixed with gravity. It cannot be remarked that any one saw him laugh, but many have seen him weep. In proportion of body, most excellent; his hands and arms delicate to behold. In speaking, very temperate, modest, and wise. A man, for his singular beauty, surpassing the children of men.

This so-called "letter" has been traced back to the eleventh century, a copy having been found in the manuscript writings of St. Anselm, archbishop of Canterbury from 1093 to 1109. The description of Jesus in this document bears a striking resemblance to one in the writings of Nicephorus, who lived early in the fourteenth century and who was the last of the Greek ecclesiastical historians.

It is now generally agreed that the Lentulus letter was written during the Middle Ages either as a deliberate forgery or as fiction. There is no probability that it is genuine. No such person as Publius Lentulus was governor or procurator of Judaea, and the style, spirit and other internal evidence all stamp it as apocryphal. It is interesting only because it is the most ancient of the many purported descriptions of the personal appearance of Jesus.

Was Jesus a Roman Citizen?

As far as we know Jesus was not a Roman citizen, as the term is generally used, although He was a Roman national or subject. Citizenship then, as now, carried with it certain rights and privileges as well as duties. Palestine in the time of Jesus had the status of a conquered province, which was divided into several principalities with varying degrees of autonomy. At that time comparatively few of the inhabitants, whether Gentiles or Jews, had acquired Roman citizenship.

Galilee, where Jesus lived, was part of a tetrarchy, which also included Peraca, and Herod Antipas was tetrarch throughout the life of Jesus. This tetrarchy was in the nature of a vassal state and the tetrarch was a puppet king with very restricted local powers. Judaea and Samaria during most of the lifetime of Jesus constituted a Roman province attached directly to the Empire and was governed by a series of procurators or governors, of whom Pontius Pilate was sixth. Very few Jews at that time were Roman citizens. Most of them probably would not have accepted Roman citizenship if it had been offered to them.

Both the Roman Republic and the Roman Empire developed from the old city-state of Rome. The only full-fledged Roman citizens were the privileged classes in the city of Rome. All members of the Roman senate had to be residents of the city, and a Roman citizen could exercise his franchise only within the limits of the capital.

In the time of Jesus the number of Roman citizens in the Empire was only a few million in a total population of about 120 million. Roman citizens outside the city of Rome enjoyed certain privileges and civil rights not enjoyed by the mere nationals. They had the right to appeal to Caesar from decisions of the local authorities, and if condemned to death could not be executed by crucifixion.

During the reign of Claudius (41 to 54 A.D.), who became emperor about twelve years after the crucifixion of Jesus, the rights of Roman citizens living outside Rome and Italy were increased and such citizens were permitted to sit as members of the Roman senate. Sometimes, as a mark of special consideration, civil rights were conferred upon entire cities and communities outside Italy. Pompey granted the protection of Roman citizenship to Tarshish (or Tarsus, a city of Cilicia), which was confirmed by Julius Caesar.

Thus Paul, as well as his father before him, was a Roman citizen. In connection with the arrest of Paul and Silas at Philippi, the chief city of that part of Macedonia and a colony, Acts 16:35-38 says, "And when it was day, the magistrates sent the serjeants, saying, Let those men go. And the keeper of the prison told this saying to Paul, The magistrates have sent to let you go: now therefore depart, and go in peace. But Paul said unto them, They have beaten us openly uncondemned, being Romans, and have cast [us] into prison; and now do they thrust us out privily? nay verily; but let them come themselves and fetch us out. And the serjeants told these words unto the magistrates: and they feared, when they heard that they were Romans."

From Acts 22 we learn that Paul was free born in Tarsus and that his parents were Jews. The chief captain who ordered Paul bound and scourged at Jerusalem admitted that he himself had paid a great sum for citizenship. Historians inform us that the sale of civil rights to foreigners and nationals was at that time the source of considerable revenue to the Roman government.

In Philippians 3:5 the Apostle to the Gentiles (Paul) says he was of "the stock of Israel, of the tribe of Benjamin, a Hebrew of the Hebrews." Thus it is clear that Jews living in the Roman provinces were permitted to enjoy the status of Roman citizens and what was known as "the freedom of the city."

Paul finally appealed directly to Caesar in Rome, which was one of the prerogatives of Roman citizenship in certain cases. According to tradition, when Paul was later condemned to death in Rome, he could not be scourged and crucified because he was a Roman citizen; but Peter, who was not a Roman citizen, suffered both of these humiliations and tortures.

Jesus was not a Roman citizen, but lived and died a Roman national. Not being a Roman citizen, He could not appeal Pilate's decision, and He was scourged and crucified as a Roman subject without civil rights.

Some have argued that Isaiah was writing about his own wife and Son and not about Jesus and Mary. Is this true?

While some have argued that Isaiah was referring to his own wife and son as types of Mary and Jesus, could any woman, even Isaiah's wife, conceiving and bearing according to the normal laws of nature represent the mother of Immanuel? Isaiah's own son, Maher-Shalal-Hash-Baz (whose name was to symbolize the successful Assyrian conquest of Damascus and Samaria) was naturally conceived. It was equally unlikely that Immanuel was to be the son of Ahaz, since in that case the king could easily prevent the sign from coming to pass, simply by giving the child a different name. We never hear of a child of either Isaiah or Ahaz who bore the name Immanuel. Furthermore, the titles given Immanuel in Isaiah 9:6, especially, "the Mighty God," could not be applied metaphorically to any child other than Jesus Christ. Thus, the reference to Mary and Jesus in Isaiah is at once directly and properly literal.

In Luke 2:21-51 we read of the circumcision, purification and redemption of the first-born. What is the Old Testament significance of each event?

God's history is honored in the circumcision of Jesus, the redemption of the first-born and the purification of Mary. Jesus was circumcised on the eighth day as prescribed by law (Genesis 17:12) as a sign of the covenant. He was given His name and was destined to be the salvation of the world. The purification of Mary was required thirty-three days after the circumcision (Leviticus 12:8). Mary gave the offering of the poor, two doves or pigeons, instead of a lamb, plus a dove or pigeon. The redemption of the first-born (Exodus 13:2, 12-16 and Numbers 18:16) was that the first-born belonged to God. It symbolized that the child was being re-purchased for five shekels.

The media always depicts Joseph as much older than Mary. Is this true?

The age of neither Mary nor Joseph is given in the Bible. The common belief that Joseph was considerably older than Mary is only a general inference from the Gospel narratives and is not based upon any particular passage.

An association of two facts undoubtedly suggested that Mary was quite young when she was espoused to Joseph. First, in Palestine girls matured rather young and were generally married in their middle teens. Second, "virgin" is used in the English Bible to render Hebrew and Geek words meaning young unmarried woman.

Although Mary is mentioned as being still alive at the time of the crucifixion, Joseph is not mentioned after the time that Jesus, at the age of twelve, was lost from His parents among the crowds in the temple at Jerusalem. It is presumed that Joseph was already dead when Jesus began His public ministry.

How were Jesus and John the Baptist related?

In Luke 1:36 the angel Gabriel, in speaking with Mary, is quoted as referring to Elizabeth as "thy cousin" in the King James Version of the Bible. If Elizabeth and Mary were first cousins, then their sons, John and Jesus, were second cousins. But the Greek word rendered *cousin* here probably means relative and it is rendered relative in the more current translations of the Bible. Consequently the degree of relationship between Jesus and John the Baptist cannot be determined for certain.

The account in Luke 1 suggests that John was six months older than Jesus. There is nothing in the Bible to indicate that Jesus and John were personally acquainted before Jesus went from Galilee to Jordan to be baptized by John.

Why was John the Baptist taken for Elijah?

The belief that the prophet Elijah would return to earth as the herald of the Messiah was based largely on Malachi 4:5 & 6, the last two verses of the Old Testament, which reads, "Behold, I am going to send you Elijah the prophet before the coming of the great and terrible day of the Lord. And he will restore the hearts of the fathers to their children, and the hearts of the children to their fathers, lest I come and smite the land with a curse."

The author of Malachi is believed to have lived during the Persian period about 450 B.C. Long before the birth of Jesus the belief that Elijah would return as the forerunner of the ideal king had become an integral part of the Messianic hope among the Jews. Elijah, one of the outstanding figures in the Old Testament, lived in the ninth century B.C. and was the prophet of zeal and fire and the worker of miracles. In the New Testament, according to Luke 1:17, the angel Gabriel told Zacharias that his unborn son John should "go as a forerunner before Him (the Lord) to turn the hearts of the fathers back to the children, and the disobedient to the attitude of the righteous; so as to make ready a people prepared for the Lord."

References to John's raiment of camel's hair, the leather girdle about his loins, and his food of locusts and wild honey, are an obvious attempt to portray John the Baptist as a "second Elijah." When the Jews sent priests and Levites from Jerusalem to ask John whether he was Elijah or the Prophet, according to John 1:21, he answered, "I am not" and "No." But Matthew 11:14 quotes Jesus as saying, after He had referred to John as the messenger of whom the prophets had spoken: "And if you care to accept it, he himself is Elijah who was to come." Luke 9:7-9 tells us that Herod the tetrarch, after he had beheaded John the Baptist, was perplexed "because it was said by some that John had risen from the dead, and by some that Elijah had appeared."

Jesus Himself seems to have been mistaken by some to be Elijah. When Jesus asked His disciple, "Who do the people say that I am?" they answered, "John the Baptist; but some say, Elijah; and other say that one of the prophets is risen again."

In the transfiguration as recorded in Matthew 17:1-3, Moses and Elijah appeared talking with Jesus. Later in the same chapter (verses 10-13) the disciples asked Jesus: "Why then do the scribes say that Elijah must come first?" Jesus answered: "Elijah is coming and will restore all things; but I say to you, that Elijah already came, and they did not recognize him, but did to him whatever they wished." Matthew adds: "Then the disciples understood that He had spoken to them about John the Baptist." Even at the crucifixion Elijah was in the minds of many present. In Matthew 27:46-50 Jesus cries out "Eli, Eli, lama sabachthani?" (My God, My God, why hast thou forsaken me?) and some thought He was calling for Elijah while the rest said "Let us see whether Elijah will come to save Him."

Did Jesus say we should be content with our wages?

Although the quotation is often attributed to Jesus, it was John the Baptist who told the soldiers to be content with their wages. According to Luke 3:14, when the soldiers asked what they should do, John said to them, "Do not take money from anyone by force, or accuse anyone falsely, and *be content with your wages.*"

How could Jesus (as Luke 2:40 states) increase in wisdom since God is omniscient?

Luke 2:40 tells us that Jesus "continued to grow and become strong, increasing in wisdom." A similar question concerning His lack of knowledge may be asked about Matthew 24:36 (which references the end times): "But of that day and hour no one knows, not even the angels of heaven, nor the Son, but the Father alone." How could Jesus not know since He is God?

These questions pose an interesting problem; but they are not an irreconcilable ones. They are not solvable by simply separating Jesus' divine and human natures. The Council of Chalcedon in 451 determined that we could not change, divide, mix or separate the two natures of Christ.

Roman Catholic theologians solve the problem with the "accommodation" theory of St. Aquinas; that is Jesus accommodated His omniscience. The dilemma with this is, if Jesus knew the hour, but accommodated by saying, as He did in Matthew 24:36, that He did not know the hour, He would not be telling the truth and therefore would not be sinless.

Protestant theologians solve the problem by "philosophically" distinguishing between, but not separating, Jesus' human and divine natures. One may argue this is merely a difference in semantics, until one considers the fact that Luke 2:40 also indicates that He grew and became strong. This same question can be rephrased to ask how Jesus, being God, who is omnipotent and immutable, could grow and become strong? Again, distinguishing between He two natures solves the problem.

Did Jesus baptize?

Whether Jesus Himself personally baptized with water is not made entirely clear. John 3:22 says: "After these things Jesus and His disciples came into the land of Judea; and there He was spending time with them, and baptizing." In John 3:25-26: "There arose therefore a discussion on the part of John's disciples with a Jew about purification. And they came to John, and said to him, 'Rabbi, He who was with you beyond the Jordan, to whom you have born witness, behold, He is baptizing, and all are coming to Him.'"

While this seems to indicate that Jesus did baptize, John 4:1-2 says: "When therefore the Lord knew that the Pharisees had heard that Jesus was making and baptizing more disciples than John (although Jesus Himself was not baptizing but His disciples were)." The Synoptic Gospels, Matthew, Mark and Luke are silent on the subject.

Apparently the Pharisees expected the Messiah to baptize, perhaps from certain hints in the prophets, for John 1:25 says: "And they asked him (John the Baptist) and said to him, 'Why then are you baptizing, if you are not the Christ, nor Elijah, nor the Prophet?'" John answered that he baptized with water, but that there stood among them one who "baptized with the Holy Spirit" (John 1:33).

Matthew 3:11 quotes John as saying: "As for me, I baptize you in water for repentance, but He who is coming after me is mightier than I, and I am not even fit to remove His sandals; He Himself will baptize you with the Holy Spirit and fire." Luke 12:49-50 says: ""I have come to cast fire upon the earth; and how I wish it were already kindled! But I have a baptism to undergo, and how distressed I am until it is accomplished."

According to Mark 10:38-39: "And they said to Him, 'We are able.' And Jesus said to them, 'The cup that I drink you shall drink; and you shall be baptized with the baptism with which I am baptized.'" I would conclude from these passages that, while Jesus did Himself personally administer the rite of baptism with water in the early days of His ministry, it was merely a temporary practice. It was not a vital part of His mission for Him to continue to personally administer baptism with water.

Did Jesus ever offer sacrifices?

There is nothing in the Bible to indicate the Jesus Himself ever offered sacrifices according to the Law of Moses. But an argument from silence is never conclusive.

It was possible for an individual Israelite to observe the Mosaic Law and still go through life without ever being obligated to offer sacrifices for himself. However, since the Bible is clear that Jesus was sinless there would be no need for Him to offer a sacrifice. Instead the Bible tells us, He Himself became the supreme sacrifice for all, who through the grace of God, come to Him.

The New Testament makes it clear that Joseph and Mary offered the sacrifice required by Levitical Law when Jesus was a child. According to Luke 2:24: "And to offer a sacrifice according to what was said in the Law of the Lord, "a pair of turtledoves or two young pigeons.'" This was a personal sin offering required of a woman who bore a child. Leviticus 12:8 states: "But if she cannot afford a lamb, then she shall take two turtledoves or two young pigeons, the one for a burnt offering; and the other for a sin offering; and the priest shall make atonement for her and she shall be clean."

How does the term Messiah differ from the term Christ?

Messiah is from the Hebrew word meaning anointed. At first it was used simply as the title in the sense of the Anointed One. I Samuel 24:5-6 states: "And began about afterward that David's conscience bothered him because he had cut off the edge of Saul's robe. So he said to his men, "Far be it from me because of the Lord that I should do this thing to my lord, the Lord's anointed, to stretch out my hand against him, since he is the Lord's anointed."

Priests and prophets, as well as kings, were anointed in Israel as a sign of their elevation to high functions. In Psalms 105:15 the term is applied to the patriarchs as the chosen people. The Lord suffered no man to do the wrong, even reproved kings for their sake, and said: "Do not touch My anointed ones, And do My prophets no harm."

Later the prophets applied the term Messiah or the Anointed One to an ideal king, a descendant of David, who was referred to as the Deliverer, the Prince of Peace, the Son of God, a Branch from the stem of David, the Elect of the Lord, the Servant of Jehovah, the Savior, the Everlasting King, and the spiritual and perhaps temporal ruler who would at some undetermined time deliver the broken and scattered tribes of Israel. The conviction that such a Messiah would come was firmly fixed and widespread among the Jews by the time of Jesus' birth.

In the King James Version of the Old Testament, Messiah is used only in Daniel 9:25-26, which reads: "So you are to know and discern that from the issuing of a decree to restore and rebuild Jerusalem until Messiah the Prince, there will be seven weeks and sixty-two weeks; it will be built again, with plaza and moat, even in times of distress. Then after the sixty-two weeks the Messiah will be cut off and have nothing, and the people of the prince who is to come will destroy the city and the sanctuary. And its end will come with a flood; even to the end there will be war; desolations are determined."

Except in two instances in the New Testament, "Christos," the Greek equivalent, renders the word for Messiah from which came Latin "Christus" and English "Christ." John 1:41 says: "He (that is Andrew) found first his own brother Simon, and said to him 'We have found the Messiah' (which translated means Christ)." According to John 4:25, the woman of Samaria at Jacob's well said to Jesus: "I know that Messiah is coming (He who is called Christ); when that One comes, He will declare all things to us."

John Wycliffe and later translators, following the Latin Vulgate, use the form "Messias" in these two passages. The form Messiah was invented by the translators of the Geneva Bible in 1560, perhaps because they thought it looked more Hebraic, and it eventually became the prevalent form of the word in English. "Messianic" (generally pronounced mess-i-ANN-ick) is an adjective that means pertaining to the Messiah, and was formed from the older form "Messias."

What does the word beatitude mean?

Beatitude is not in the English Bible. It is an Anglicized form of the Latin "beatitudo," meaning happiness or blessedness. The Latin adjective is "beatus," which means happy or blessed.

Since the 16th century at least the pleural form Beatitudes has been applied to Matthew 5:3-11, which are the nine verses in the Sermon on the Mount that begin with the words "Blessed are." A similar introductory formula is found in Psalms 1:1, 41:1, and 65:4, which begin, "Blessed is the man that," "Blessed is he that" and "Blessed is the man whom."

What did Jesus mean by the "eye of a needle"? Many Bible students have attempted to prove that when Jesus said, "It is easier for a camel to go through the eye of a needle, then for a rich man to enter the kingdom of heaven," the phrase eye of a needle referred to a small gate that was opened in the great gate of an Oriental city when the latter was closed for the night. They say it is difficult, but possible, for a camel to pass through such a gate. There is no positive evidence to support this theory and it is apparently without foundation, although many students of the Scriptures accept it.

This figurative use of the eye of a needle recurs in all three of the Synoptic Gospels, Matthew 19:24, Mark 10:25, and Luke 18:25. Some writers believe that Jesus wished really to point out the difference between what is possible with men and what is possible with God. It is recorded that the statement of Jesus astonished the disciples. They asked: "Who then can be saved?" Jesus replied: "With men it is impossible, but not with God: for with God all things are possible."

It is more probable, however, that Jesus is illustrating something actually impossible, rich man meaning a person selfishly bound up in his riches. That such was the meaning of Jesus is becoming more and more the accepted theory among Bible scholars. In Mark 10:24 it is recorded that Jesus said: "How hard is it for them that trust in riches to enter into the kingdom of God." After relating the parable of the sower, Jesus, according to Mark 9:14 said, "And the cares of this world, and the deceitfulness of riches, and the lusts of other things entering in, choke the word, and it becomes unfruitful." Luke 18:22 tells us that Jesus told the ruler who was rich but who had kept the Commandments: "You lack one thing; sell all that you have, and distribute to the poor, and you shall have treasure in heaven." There are other passages in the Gospels illustrating the same attitude toward worldly riches.

It is probable that the saying about the camel and the needle's eye was proverbial already in the time of Jesus. Mohammed used it six centuries later. The Koran says: "The impious shall find the gates of heaven shut, nor shall he enter till a camel pass through the eye of a needle." This is another way of saying that the impious shall not enter at all. Some suppose the Greek words for camel and rope were confused, and cable for camel occurs in a few versions of Scripture, but earlier texts do not support the theory, which is generally rejected. Needle occurs nowhere else in the Bible, although needlework does.

Why is Jesus called the Good Shepherd?

We read of Jesus as The Good Shepherd in John 10:11 and 14 because, He gives His life for His sheep, and He knows His sheep and they know Him. Jesus is also called The Good Physician in Mark 2:17. In the New Testament more than thirty different names, titles and descriptive phrases are applied to Jesus. The most common are: Emmanuel; Jesus of Nazareth; the Nazarene; Messiah (Messias); Son of David; Son of God; Son of Man; Christ; Jesus Christ; Christ Jesus; Lord; Master; Christ the Lord; Lord's Christ; Lord Jesus Christ; Lord Jesus; King of the Jews; Lamb of God; Son of the Highest; Savior; Redeemer; Light of the World; Holy One of God; Just One; Holy One; Rock; and the Comforter. Although many refer to the Holy Spirit as the "Comforter," actually Jesus referred to the Holy Spirit as "another Comforter" (see John 14:16).

Why did Jesus call Himself the Son of Man?

In the Gospels Jesus refers to Himself more than eighty times as the Son of Man. Authorities differ widely as to why He chose that title. Jesus often permitted Himself to be called the Son of God by others, but He applied that title to Himself only by implication. He seems to have used Son of Man very much as He used I or as He might have used His own name in the third person.

A Hebrew term rendered son of man occurs in the singular and in the pleural in Psalms, Ecclesiastes, Proverbs, Isaiah, Jeremiah, Ezekiel, Job, Daniel and other parts of the Old Testament. There, except in Daniel, it generally means a human being, a mortal, mere man, or frail humanity. Ezekiel, conscious of his own mortality and frailty, applies son of man to himself about ninety times.

Some authorities suppose that Jesus, out of modesty and humiliation, referred to Himself as the son of man merely in the general sense of that term as it is used in the Old Testament. But the Greek term rendered son of man in the New Testament has no clear and obvious counterpart in Aranaic, the language that Jesus is supposed to have spoken. Aramaic "bar enash" signifies son of man only in the literal sense. For that reason even the authenticity of the phrase in the Gospels has been questioned.

Other authorities suppose this title had some special Messianic significance, although there is no positive evidence that it was so understood by the Jews in the time of Jesus. Psalms 8:4 says, "What is man, that Thou dost take thought of him? And the son of man, that Thou dost care for him?" In Daniel 7:13 and 14 the prophet saw in the night visions one like the Son of Man who came with the clouds and to whom all glory was given. These passages were sometimes interpreted as alluding to the Messiah and may have been a source of the title as used by Jesus. When Jesus says in Matthew 16:28, "Truly I say to you, there are some of those who are standing here who shall not taste death until they see the Son of Man coming in His kingdom," He is undoubtedly alluding to the passage in Daniel just cited.

In Mark 14:62, in answer to the high priest's question whether He was the Christ, Jesus said, "I am; and you shall see the Son of Man sitting at the right hand of power and coming with the clouds of heaven." In Daniel, one like the son of man is indefinite and appears to denote that this vision was in human form as contrasted with the brute forms in the preceding visions. But in the Gospels, where the son of man is used continually and only by Jesus, the title is individualized and definitely identified with Jesus Himself.

Jesus may have adopted this particular phrase to hide His identity with the Messiah from some while the same time to reveal it to others. Son of man is specifically identified with the Messiah in the Apocryphal Book of Enoch, but it is not certain that those writings antedate Jesus. If Enoch was in circulation at that time, Jesus may have obtained the title from that book, which is quoted in The General Epistle of Jude, generally ascribed to Jesus' brother of that name.

Does Sermon on the Mount occur in the Bible?

The word sermon, a word of Latin origin and signifying "talk" or "discourse," is found nowhere in the Bible. The name Sermon on the Mount was given to the fifth, sixth and seventh chapters of Matthew as early as the fourth century, when St. Augustine wrote his commentary on the subject.

These chapters open with, "And when He saw the multitudes, He went up on the mountain: and after He sat down, His disciples came to Him. And opening His mouth He began to teach them, saying," and are followed with, "And when He had come down from the mountain, great multitudes followed Him."

Many authorities suppose that the Sermon on the Mount is largely a compilation of the sayings of Jesus that were uttered at different times in different places and that were later collected and arranged as if they compose one discourse. This is based upon parallel sayings in other connections in the Gospels and certain internal evidence that they are not preserved in their original connection. A somewhat similar arrangement of the sayings of Jesus is recorded in Luke

6:20-49. This is sometimes called the Sermon on the Plain, because in Luke 6:17 Jesus is represented as standing in the plain when He spoke.

Is the mustard seed the least of all seeds?

In Matthew 13:31 and 32, Jesus is quoted as saying, "The kingdom of heaven is like a mustard seed, which a man took and sowed in his field; and this is smaller than all other seeds; but when it is full-grown, it is larger than the garden plants, and becomes a tree, so that the birds of the air come and nest in its branches." In Matthew 17:20 Jesus says, "If you have faith as a mustard seed, you shall say to this mountain, "Move from here to there," and it shall move; and nothing shall be impossible to you."

Mustard and mustard seed occur nowhere in the Bible except in these passages in the corresponding passages in Mark and Luke. Although the mustard plant is compared to a tree, it is believed that herb, not the so-called mustard tree, is referred to. In Palestine this annual herb, a common source of spice, often attains a height of 10 or 12 feet and certain birds do actually nest in its branches.

The mustard seed is not literally the smallest of all seeds, but it was so regarded in popular parlance. Among the rabbis "the quantity of a mustard seed" was the proverbial way of expressing the smallest possible quantity, and in the Koran, Mohammed employed the same figure of speech.

Did Jesus say, "The spirit is willing, but the flesh is weak?"

This is a popular version of a saying of Jesus in Matthew 26:41 and in Mark 14:38. The exact words of the verse as recorded by Matthew are, "Keep watching and praying, that you may not enter into temptation: the spirit is willing, but the flesh is weak." Jesus uttered these words on the night of the arrest in the place called Gethsemane on the Mount of

Olives after He had asked the three disciples with Him to wait and watch while He went a stone's throw away to pray, but returned an hour later to find them asleep. This particular saying was addressed to Peter.

How do the Catholic and Protestant Bibles differ?

The Catholic and Protestant Bibles do not differ in the contents of the New Testament but do differ considerably in the contents of the Old Testament. At the Council of Trent (1546-1563) the Roman Catholic church enumerated the books that should be regarded as "sacred and canonical" and consequently as parts of the Bible. This list comprises all but three (Esdras I, Esdras II and the Prayer of Manasses) of the books and portions of books which are not found in the Jewish traditions of the Old Testament and which Protestants generally refer to as the Apocrypha. Accordingly the Catholic Bible comprises all of the Old Testament books accepted as canonical by Protestants plus Tobias, Judith, Wisdom of Solomon, Ecclesiasticus, Baruch, Maccabees I, Maccabees II, and certain fragments of Esther and Daniel.

Strictly speaking, the Apocryphal books are not essential parts of the Protestant Bible, although they were formerly printed between the Testaments in nearly all Protestant editions, and the Bibles on the lecterns of the Anglican Church and the Protestant Episcopal Church have contained these books, and lessons are taken from them on certain days of the Church Year. Thus, it will be seen that the chief difference between the Catholic and Protestant Bibles is that the Catholics regard all but three of the so-called Apocryphal books and parts of books as canonical and as essential parts of the Scriptures, while the Protestants read them merely for personal inspiration and edification and do not use them to establish points of doctrine.

What does canon mean in connection with the Bible?

Canon is a Greek and Latin word meaning "rule" or "measure," such as a carpenter's rule. By extension it came to signify "a standard," "a model," "a criterion for" or "an ordinance."

The term does not occur in either the Old or the New Testament, but as early as the fourth century it began to be used in the specific sense of the biblical writings received and accepted as genuine and inspired. The sacred canon, also called the canonical books, consists of the whole list, collection or body of books of the Bible that are accepted as genuine and inspired Holy Scriptures; that is, the whole Bible from Genesis to Revelation.

But the exact books of the sacred canon are not identical for all churches and synagogues. The sacred canon for the Jews, of course, includes only the Old Testament and was fixed at an early date. The Roman Catholic canon of the whole Bible was finally fixed by the Council of Trent, which sat from 1545 to 1563, although the canon had been substantially fixed long before. The Roman Catholic sacred canon contains certain Old Testament books not accepted by the Jews and Protestants and are referred to as the Old Testament Apocrypha.

What is the Apocrypha?

Apocrypha is from a Greek word meaning "hidden." Strictly speaking, it is a plural, but in common usage it is constructed as a singular. Apocrypha was first applied to books or writings that were put away and withdrawn from general use because they were worn out or faulty copies. Next the term was applied to books regarded as unsuitable for general or public reading. Then it was applied to books containing mysterious, esoteric, secret or hidden things favored by few.

Cyril of Jerusalem, a fourth-century Syrian churchman, is believed to have been the first to apply apocrypha to biblical books of doubtful origin and authority. The original apocrypha in this sense consisted of certain books and parts of books in the Greek Septuagint that were not found in Hebrew and which the Jews did not recognize as part of their canon. Now the term is applied specifically to the following fourteen books: *Tobit, Judith,* additions to *Esther, Wisdom of Solomon, Ecclesiasticus* or *Wisdom of Jesus, Son of Sirach, Baruch, Song of the Three Children, Susanna, Bel and the Dragon, I* and *II Maccabees, I* and *II Esdras,* and the *Prayer of Manasses.*

Following Martin Luther, the Church of England gave these apocryphal books "inferior authority" and classed them as non-canonical. They are not recognized in any manner by other Protestant churches, but some read them for instruction, inspiration, and edification, although no Protestant church uses them in fixing points of doctrine.

There is also a New Testament apocrypha that is the same for Roman Catholics and Protestants. It covers a wide range of literature and contains many books and fragments of the gospels, acts and epistles. Some of the best known are: the gospels according to the Hebrews, the Egyptians, the Ebionites, Peter, Thomas, Philip, and Nicodemus; the acts of John, Peter, Thomas, Andrew and Paul; the Preaching of Peter; the Birth of Mary; the Oxyrthynchus Logia; the Agrapha; the Abgarus Letters; the Shepherd of Hermas; the Protevangelium of James; the Epistle of Paul to the Laodiceans; the Apocalypse of Peter and a number of others.

The New Testament apocrypha is for the most part distinct from the body of second century Christian Patristic writings known as the Apostolic Fathers. Most of the New Testament apocryphal books have been at one time or other regarded as canonical by one Christian sect or another. They are the source of many sacred legends and ecclesiastical traditions.

Is the Feast of the Immaculate Conception, celebrated on December 8th each year, the same as the Virgin Birth?

No it is not. These two doctrines are entirely different. Although the term Virgin Birth does not occur in the Bible, this doctrine is held by both Roman Catholics and Protestants alike and is founded on biblical passages in Matthew 1:18, 22-25, Luke 1:34-35 and the prophecy in Isaiah 7:14. This doctrine refers to the fact that Jesus was miraculously begotten of God and born of a virgin mother.

The Immaculate Conception, on the other hand, is uniquely a doctrine of the Roman Catholic Church and does not concern the birth of Jesus but rather concerns the birth of the Virgin Mary by her mother, whose name is not given in the Bible, but which traditionally was Anna. The doctrine of the Immaculate Conception holds that the Virgin Mary, by a singular privilege and grace granted by God, was preserved exempt and immaculate from all stain of original sin. All other descendants of Adam, with the exception of Jesus, have been born with original sin on their souls.

Mary, according to the doctrine of Immaculate Conception, was immune from original sin at the moment her soul was created and infused into her body. The doctrine does not, as some erroneously believe, refer to Mary's physical conception by her parents who had the usual part in the formation of her body. The doctrine of the Immaculate Conception of the Virgin Mary was a subject of controversy for about six hundred years. Finally, on December 8, 1854, Pope Pius IX proclaimed the Immaculate Conception as a dogmatic article of faith for Roman Catholics.

Does the Bible mention the Assumption of Mary that is commemorated each August 15th?

No reference to the death of Mary, the mother Jesus, is found in the Bible. Both the Roman Catholic Church and the Eastern Orthodox Church teach that the Virgin Mary was received directly into heaven. A special feast commemorates "The Assumption of the Blessed Virgin Mary" on August 15. The Assumption of Mary is the fourth and last Marian dogma of the Roman Catholic Church, having been decreed by the Pope in 1950.

The other three Marian dogmas are known as the "Mother of God," "Perpetual Virgin," and the "Immaculate Conception," the latter having been decreed by the Pope in 1854.

Assumption is derived from Latin ad, "to," and sumere, "to take," and the Assumption of the Virgin Mary refers to the assumption of her body into heaven upon her death, since she was sinless according to the third Marian dogma, the Immaculate Conception. Titian's "Assumption of the Virgin" is regarded as one of the finest oil paintings in the world. When Napoleon was looting the art treasures of Italy to enrich his galleries in Paris, this priceless canvas in the Church of the Frari at Venice was so blackened by candle smoke that the French art commissions decided that was not worth taking away.

What is the major difference between Roman Catholicism and Evangelical Protestantism?

Most people would answer this question by pointing to the different views Roman Catholics and Protestants have concerning the papacy, Mary, the saints, purgatory or the sacraments. However, these distinctive differences all stem from the doctrinal dispute over justification.

Admittedly the debate over justification suffers from a crass caricature by which the Protestant position is incompletely characterized as "justification by faith" and the Roman Catholic position is incompletely characterized as "justification by works." Popular sentiment falsely concludes that Protestants are not concerned about works and that Rome is not concerned with faith.

Roman Catholicism has always given an important and necessary place to faith in so far as justification is concerned. Moreover, Protestantism has always held that saving faith necessarily, inevitably and immediately yields the fruit of works. The difference in the two views is that in Roman Catholicism, "*Faith plus Works yields Justification*" while in Protestantism, "*Faith yields Justification plus Works.*" That is, in Roman Catholicism "*Works*" is a necessary precondition for justification. In Protestantism, "*Works*" is a necessary fruit of justification.

Protestantism holds to the vicarious atonement of Christ. It is vicarious because it is accomplished by imputation (transfer), actually a double imputation (transfer). Christ willingly bore for His people their sins that are imputed or transferred to Him. Christ is the sin-bearer for His people (the Lamb of God) who takes away (expiates) their sin and satisfies (propitiates) the demands of God's justice. The cross alone, however, does not justify. There is also a need for positive righteousness. Protestantism maintains that one is not justified only by the death of Christ but also by the life of Christ. His perfect righteousness is also imputed to those whom He redeems. Hence there is a double imputation. The sins of the redeemed are imputed to Christ on the cross, and Christ's perfect righteousness is imputed to the redeemed. Evidence of such imputed justification is then seen in the works performed by those justified.

Roman Catholicism rejects this concept of imputation and maintains that God does not consider someone righteous on the basis of some alien (Christ's) righteousness (a righteousness outside of oneself). Rome's view presupposes that the only true justness or righteousness is inherent righteousness. Hence, there is a need for a person to become righteous in him or herself first before God declares one righteous. Although Rome teaches that a person cannot become righteous without infused grace, a person is deemed righteous only when he or she has become (through works) righteous.

Given the Protestant doctrine of justification, it would be impossible to ascribe to the Roman Catholic doctrines the papacy, Mary, the saints, purgatory or the sacraments. Only under a system of justification whereby righteousness was something that was initially infused by God into the believer and then increased when the believer cooperated by specific works could such doctrines exist.

Clearly a vast theological gulf separates Roman Catholic and Protestant theology on the doctrine of justification. Unless Protestant theology rejects the principles of the Reformation, or Roman Catholic theology abandons much of the canons and decrees of the Council of Trent (especially canons 9, 10, and 11), the doctrine of justification will remain a fundamental source of division between Roman Catholicism and the Evangelical Protestant faith.

Why do artists depict Moses with horns?

Many medieval painters depicted Moses with horns protruding from his head. Michelangelo's masterpiece, the colossal figure of Moses in the Church of St. Pietro in Rome, also represents the leader of the Israelites with horns. This figure was designed for the mausoleum of Pope Julius II and was intended as a compliment to that Pope's warlike prowess. It portrays the painfully restrained wrath and majestic indignation of Moses when he descended from Mt. Sinai and found his people worshipping the golden calf.

Although the horns undoubtedly heighten the effect desired, they were really owing to a mistake in Biblical translation. In Exodus 34:29 & 30 it is stated: "And it came about when Moses was coming down from Mount Sinai (and the two tablets of the testimony were in Moses' hand as he was coming down from the mountain) that Moses did not know that the skin of his face shone because of his speaking with Him (God). So when Aaron and all the sons of Israel saw Moses, behold the skin of his face shone, and they were afraid to come near him."

In Hebrew the word for this shinning is *qaran* or *karan*, which means "rays of light darting out" or "sending forth beams." The Hebrew word for horn is *qeren*. The translators of the Latin version of the Old Testament known as the Vulgate rendered the phrase *quod cornuta esset facies sua*, which means, "his face was horned." Since horn is frequently used in the Bible for strength, the medieval artists represented Moses with horns, thinking the horns were mentioned in the Bible to symbolize power.

The error was perfectly understandable, because the Vulgate version was made in the fourth century A.D. before vowels had been introduced into Hebrew. Perhaps the original idea in Exodus about the face of Moses shining alluded to what later became known as the halo, nimbus and aureole.

Who was St. Patrick?

Contrary to popular belief, St. Patrick was not of Irish birth. He was born in Wales, and later became a bishop, teacher and missionary. He allegedly chased the "snakes" out of Ireland. Here "snakes" is implied to represent the sinful state of Ireland prior to the reforming teaching and scholarship of St. Patrick. Since then Ireland has been known as the isle of "Scholars and Saints." A little know fact is that there were more Irish who signed our Declaration of Independence that any other nationality. March 17 has been set aside each year to honor Ireland's patron saint.

Does the Bible require priests to be celibate?

Celibacy was unknown to the ancient Israelites and would probably have been incomprehensible to them. To be fruitful, multiply and replenish the earth (Genesis 1:28) was one of the first pre-Mosaic commandments given to mankind.

Judaism has always emphasized the duty of building a home and rearing a family. The rabbis have always taught that the celibate life is an unblessed life.

Israel from the first had a married priesthood. Not only did the Levites and priests marry, but the office passed down from father to son. By the Mosaic law, the tribe of Levi was set apart as the priestly class in the theocracy of Israel. Marriage laws and customs for the Levites and priests were stricter than for others because of the importance of preserving the priestly lineage.

There is no evidence in the Bible that even the vow (to separate from certain worldly things and to consecrate oneself to God – see Numbers 6:1-8) taken by the Nazarite prohibited the marriage relation. Samson, a Nazarite, was married. Certain prophets, priests and other individuals may have taken the vow of celibacy in ancient Israel, and this practice appears to have been quite common among the Jews in Palestine in the time of Jesus.

Were the early followers of Jesus celibates?

There was a sect of Jews at that time called Essenes who abstained from marriage in violation of the law of Moses and the usual Jewish conception of life. Although the Essenes are not mentioned by name in the Bible, it is believed that many of their teachings had a profound influence upon the doctrines of John the Baptist, Jesus' disciples and many of the early Christians. Some authorities even suppose that the early Christian church in Palestime absorbed almost the entire Essene sect.

John the Baptist is supposed to have been a celibate. Of the twelve disciples of Jesus, there is no definite evidence that any of them was married except Peter whose "wife's mother" is referred to in Matthew 7:14 as well as in Mark and Luke. Eusebius records a tradition that Peter's wife accompanied him to Rome and suffered martyrdom a short time after her husband Peter did. Phillip the evangelist, whom Paul visited at Caesarea and who had four daughters who did prophesy, was probably not the same person as Phillip, one of the Twelve Apostles.

It is also questionable whether Paul ever married. Some have argued that Paul's (then named Saul) involvement in the stoning of Stephen, and in voting against many Christians as recorded in Acts 26:10, infers that he must have been a member of the Sanhedrin, whose membership required one to be a married male. Paul, nevertheless, held up absolute celibacy as an ideal. He did not require celibacy on the part of Christians but regarded marriage as perhaps necessary and a lesser evil than licentiousness (I Corinthians 7).

Were the priests in the early Christian Church married?

In the early days of the Christian Church the clergy were permitted to marry. The growth of celibacy, first as a custom and then as a rule of discipline, was gradual among the clergy of the Roman Catholic Church. Even in modern times some Eastern churches under the jurisdiction of Rome have had a married priesthood. Many bishops and priests, perhaps in imitation of St. Paul, voluntarily began to practice celibacy at an early date. Second marriages of priests began to be questioned; then marriage of priests was restricted to virgins.

The first church council that definitely forbade marriage to the higher clergy was the local synod of Elvira in 305 A.D. Eighty years later in 385 A.D., Pope Siricius issued a decree enjoining strict celibacy upon all bishops, priests and deacons. He insisted on the immediate separation of those who were married and prescribed expulsion as the penalty for disobedience. This may be regarded as the real beginning of universal compulsory sacerdotal celibacy in the Roman Catholic Church as a rule of discipline. This rule was later extended to sub deacons.

For several centuries, however, the rules against marriage were widely violated both openly and secretly by priests and bishops. In the eleventh century several Popes turned their attention to the question and took stringent measures to enforce the injunctions against marriage among the clergy. Pope Gregory VII, who was Pope from 1073 to 1085, especially distinguished himself in this respect. He enforced the celibacy rules so stringently that he is still often erroneously credited with being their author. The word celibacy does not occur in the Bible but it is derived from the Latin *caelebs*, meaning unmarried or single.

How many popes are mentioned in the Bible?

The Roman Catholic Church regards the Apostle Peter as the first Bishop of Rome and accordingly as the first pope. He is the only person whose name appears in the list of popes who is known definitely to be mentioned in the bible.

According to a list generally accepted by Roman Catholic authorities, Pope Benedict XVI, who assumed the tiara in 2005, is the 265th pope. There is, however, a wide difference of opinion among Roman Catholics themselves as to the exact number. Many names on the list are doubtful.

According to a tradition, St. Linus succeeded St. Peter as pope and reigned twelve years (67-79 A.D.). St. Irenaeus, who wrote during the latter part of the second century, was of the opinion that the second pope, was the Linus mentioned by St. Paul in II Timothy 4:21.

Although Roman Catholics regard St. Peter as the first pope and head of the Roman Catholic Church, there have been no later popes named Peter. It is supposed that no later popes assumed the name because they felt it would be presumptuous to style themselves Peter II, Peter III, etc.

There have been many popes named John and Paul, but none named Matthew or Luke, and only one named Mark. Each pope changes his name when he assumes the pontificate. This custom is said to have grown up after Sergius IV (who sat in the papal chair from 1099 to 1012 A.D.) abandoned his own homely name in favor of a more dignified one. Originally he was known as Peter Bucca Porci (Peter's Pig Snout) and he took the name Sergius IV because his surname was too plain and because he feared that it might be deemed arrogance on his part to style himself Peter II.

What is the legend of Santa Lucia?

The Feast of Santa Lucia is celebrated all over Sweden and Norway on December 13. Yet, no one knows for sure why a 4th. Century Sicilian saint came to be so revered in Scandinavia.

The tradition, which can be traced to Italy, honors a young wealthy Christian bride-to-be who gave away her dowry to the poor, an act which angered her prospective groom and caused him to report her Christian religion to the Roman authorities. She was condemned to death by fire.

Legend has it that just before she died an intense inner light transformed Lucia and everyone present fell prostrate. Thus Lucia, a sign of light and hope to the poor died, illuminated by a heavenly glow, on December 13 in A.D.304.

In actuality, Lucia was probably a victim of the wave of persecution of Christians that occurred late in the reign of the Roman emperor Diocletian. References to her are found in early Roman sacramentaries and at Syracuse in an inscription dating from AD 400.

The Lucia legend spread to Sweden at a time of great famine. In the province of Vanern, a large vessel appeared on the lake and at its helm stood a maiden dressed in a gleaming white robe. Believed to be Santa Lucia, she guided the ship along the lakeshore, distributing food to the poor and hungry. The ship disappeared as soon as its mission was completed.

Santa Lucia festivities, with pageantry and good food, mark the first day of the Scandinavian Christmas season that begins on December 13 and lasts one month until January 13. Santa Lucia day begins very early in the morning on December 13 in Scandinavian homes. The oldest daughter of the house, usually dresses in a long white gown, dons a crown of evergreens and lighted candles on her head, sings the beautiful Italian song "Santa Lucia," and serves special Lucia cakes and warm drinks to the rest of the family who are still in bed.

What is a sacrament?

A classic definition of a sacrament states that it is an outward and visible sign of an inward and spiritual grace. This definition summarizes the teaching of the early Fathers of the Church, notably St, Augustine, and the medieval scholastic theologians. It would be acceptable to most Christian theologians today, with the following amendment: a sacrament is distinguished from other sacred signs by its express institution, whether by word or by exemplary action by Christ Himself.

Who may perform a sacrament?

A sacrament is efficacious (capable of producing the desired effect) only when it is performed in and by the Church acting through recognized priests, ministers or agents who intend to act for the Church. Apart from the context of corporate Church life, a sacrament is meaningless, if not, more extremely, a suspicious piece of magic. To be a Christian involves more than a personal faith in the redeeming act of God in Christ. It demands incorporation into the community where the effects of Christ's redemption in reconciliation and charity may be actualized and nurtured.

An individual cannot perform a sacrament for himself; it requires at least one other person. While a sacrament is a visible token of God's free favor and grace, it is also an instrument whereby the individual is made a member or participant in a covenant community (the Church) and ordered by its disciplines and responsibilities.

Catholics and Protestants differ in their emphasis upon the way in which sacraments convey divine grace. Catholics stress the objective efficacy of the sacraments (*ex opere operato*, basically the sacrament works by itself) when duly performed with sincere intention by an authorized person, in union with Peter, using the proper form, words and elements of the sacrament. Protestants tend to emphasize the subjective conditions of penitence and faith of the individual, or the individual's family, as a condition of receiving beneficially the promise of grace proclaimed by the Word of God and offered with the sacramental signs. There is no necessary contradiction in these approaches as both view the efficacy of the sacrament as due solely to the blessing of Christ, and to the work of the Holy Spirit, which is promised to those who in faith rightly participate.

How many sacraments are there?

The word sacrament historically was used for something sacred. The Latin term *sacramentum* was used to translate the New Testament word for mystery. In a broad sense all religious rites and ceremonies were called sacraments. In time, the word sacrament took on a more precise and narrow meaning. A sacrament became defined as a visible sign by which God offers His promise of grace in an outward form. Outward signs seal and confirm the covenant promises of God. The sacraments consist of some visible element such as water, bread, or wine; a definite activity ordained by God in association with the sign; and a redeeming benefit given to the believer.

The Roman Catholic Church set the number of sacraments at seven. They are Baptism, Confirmation, Eucharist (or the Lord's Supper), Penance, Matrimony, Holy Orders, and Extreme Unction (which now includes anointing of the sick). Historic Protestantism limited the sacraments to two: Baptism and the Lord's Supper. Although Protestants recognize other rites such as marriage as special ordinances of God, they are not recognized as attaining the level of sacraments. Sacraments are limited to those ordinances directly instituted by Christ, to those ordinances that are by their very nature significant, to those ordinances designed to be perpetual, and to those ordinances designed to signify, instruct, and seal the believers who receive them in faith.

The sacraments are real means of grace that convey the promises of God. Their power does not reside in the elements themselves, but in God, whose signs they are. Nor does their power depend upon the character or the faith of those who administer them, but on the integrity of God.

The sacraments are nonverbal forms of communication. They were never intended to stand-alone without reference to the Word of God. Sacraments confirm the Word of God so that the administering of the sacraments and the preaching of the Word go together.

Martin Luther attacked Rome's understanding of the sacraments and asserted that there were but three: baptism, the bread, and penance. Luther later recognized only two sacraments, baptism and the bread. It is only in these two, Luther wrote, that we have the divinely instituted sign plus the divine promise of forgiveness.

Huldrych Zwingli had misgivings about the word sacrament. He saw sacraments as signifying allegiance (an oath) by believers to the church, rather than an allegiance of God to believers. For Zwingli, Baptism represented a public acknowledgment that a child is a member of the household of God. Zwingli argued that baptism is the New Testament equivalent of Old Testament circumcision, yet more inclusive since it embraces male and female infants. For Zwingli, attendance at the Lord's Supper was a declaration of loyalty to the community, the church. The Lord's Supper is a memorial of a historic event that established the Church and a public acknowledgment of the believer's allegiance to the church. Zwingli used a military analogy. A Swiss soldier wears a white cross as evidence of his public allegiance to the Confederacy. A Christian publicly demonstrates his allegiance to the church by baptism and subsequently by participating in the Lord's Supper.

Martin Luther, a former lawyer, regarding Christ's death as a token of trustworthiness and the grace of God, used the idea of a testament. A testament (as in a last will and testament) involves promises that become operational only after the death of the person who makes the promises. The Lord's Supper proclaims that the promises of grace and forgiveness are in effect. By proclaiming the death of Christ, the church affirms that the promises of forgiveness and eternal life are effective for the faithful.

What are the various Christian views on the sacrament of the Eucharist or the Lord's Supper?

The sacrament of the Lord's Supper has been of major importance to Christian worship. What did Jesus mean when He said, "This is my body" in Matthew 26:26? Cyril of Jerusalem regarded the bread and the wine as somehow really changing to the body and blood of Christ. Paschasius Radbertus, in support of John of Demascus who simply affirmed the mystery of the transformation of the elements, was also convinced of the physical reality and spiritual importance of the fact that the bread and the wine become the body and blood of Christ. Yet Radbertus provided no real explanation of how this transformation took place. Ratranmus of Corbie argued that the elements were merely symbols of the body and blood. The difference was in the way in which the believer perceived the elements and not in the elements themselves. The elements remained unchanged, but the believer could perceive a deeper spiritual meaning as a result of the consecration of the elements. Candidus of Fulda stated the purpose of the Lord's Supper is to nourish and bring to perfection the church. He argued that the phrase in Matthew 26:26 refers to the church as the body of Christ.

This issue of the real presence was especially controversial during the Reformation and continues today. Huldrych Zwingli maintained that the Lord's Supper is a "naked sign," a "nude symbol" or but a memorial of Christ's suffering and is not a sacrifice. For Zwingli, the words, "This is my body," cannot be taken literally and thus there is no presence (real, physical or spiritual) at the Lord's Supper. It is a token to remember Christ by until His return. Zwingli argued there are numerous passages in Scripture where "is" cannot be take literally and must be taken figuratively or metaphorically.

Both Luther and Calvin rejected the Roman Catholic view of transubstantiation, which Rome explains with metaphysical categories (substance and accidents) borrowed from Aristotle. (Substance is the essence of an item while accidents refers to the outward or surface appearance of the item.) Yet both Luther and Calvin argued for a real presence and thus also differed with Zwingli.

Martin Luther insisted that the body and blood of Christ are truly present but that they are supernaturally in, under and through the elements; much like the heat in a poker that is taken from the fire. The elements remain both in substance and accidents. This still left Luther with the problem that the accidents remain hidden to the senses.

John Calvin also insisted on the real presence of Christ. To those who reduced the sacrament to a naked sign, Calvin insisted on a substantial presence of Christ. He differed with Luther in that what Calvin meant by the term substantial was real and not physical. For Calvin the person of Christ is omnipresent. Although Christ is absent from us in body (for His body is in heaven) He is never absent from us in Spirit.

Calvin saw in Luther's view of the Lord's Supper a form of monophysitism (a doctrine that Christ had only a divine nature and that His human nature was so sublimated to His divine nature that it ceased to exist). Calvin understood the divine nature of Christ and the human nature of Christ to stay divine and human in every respect. Lutherans and Catholics countered that Calvin's rejection of the communication of attributes involved him in Nestorianism (a doctrine that separated the divine and human natures of Christ).

Yet Calvin did not separate the two natures of Christ but distinguished them. When Christ wept, sweat, or hungered, He was in perfect unity with His divine nature, but the tears, sweat, and hunger were not divine. Jesus' human nature died on the cross, but His divine nature did not die. John Calvin insisted that the God-man is indeed ubiquitous and truly and substantially present at the Lord's Supper, but in His divine nature. Although His human nature is now in heaven it is still perfectly united to the divine nature.

This is not to suggest that in the Lord's Supper we only commune with Christ's divine nature. Where His divine nature is present, His human nature is present. When we commune with His divine nature, we commune with the whole Christ because His divine nature is still united with His human nature. Although Christ's body and blood remain in heaven, they are spiritually made present to us by Jesus' omnipresent divine nature. Wherever the divine nature of Christ is present, He is truly present.

This is consistent with Jesus' own teaching that He was going away, yet He would abide with us. When we meet Him at the Lord's Supper we commune with Him. By meeting us in His divine presence, we are brought into His human presence mystically, because His divine nature is never separated from His human nature. The divine nature leads us to the ascended Christ, and in the Lord's Supper we have a taste of heaven.

Is there a difference between a sacrament and an ordinance?

Baptists prefer to use the term ordinance rather that sacrament, since they maintain Jesus "ordained" Baptism and the Lord's Supper. They view an ordinance as an outward witness of the personal faith and commitment to Jesus Christ by the believer to the world, as opposed to a sacrament that involves an outward work that seals the inward regeneration effected by the power of the Holy Spirit.

What is the difference between a sacrament and a sacramental?

In Roman Catholic theology a sacramental is a spiritual sign instituted by the church whose effectiveness rests in the power of the custom as mediated by the church rather than on the power of the rite itself. Sacraments engage the redeeming power of Christ, while sacramentals are effective only through the intermediation of the Church. Examples of sacramentals are the blessing of holy oils, the blessing of the marriage ring, and the sign of the cross.

Does Dan Brown's book and the movie The Da Vinci Code, have a strong argument for concluding Jesus and Mary Magdalene were husband and wife?

Sales of this fictional story presently exceed 35 million copies, mainly because people are interested in religion and spirituality. It matters not if Dan Brown has the facts wrong. Unfortunately most people don't know enough about the life of Christ to realize that The Da Vinci Code is full of falsehoods. As an action-suspense story, it is engaging and entertaining, but at times implausible.

Most art experts have stated that Brown gets almost nothing correct about the life of Leonardo da Vinci, that he misstates the size of one of the artist's paintings by a full 18 inches, and has one of his characters referring to him as "da Vinci" when true experts always say "Leonardo." "Da Vinci" simply means "of Vinci." If his Leonardo da Vinci research is so shoddy, what's to say his religious fact-finding is any better.

Good authors write with authoritative voices and Brown has a talent for this. For example on page 234 of The Da Vinci Code, Brown has an "expert" on the Holy Grail saying, "The Dead Sea Scrolls were found in the 1950's *(and)* in addition to telling the true Grail story, these documents speak of Christ's ministry in very human terms." The facts (which would not be known by the average reader) are that the Dead Sea Scrolls were found in 1947, they do not mention the Grail story and they never speak of Christ or Christianity at all.

Brown states that he researched the life of Mary Magdalene as it was recorded in canonical Gospels (Matthew, Mark, Luke and John) as well as the apocryphal gospels of Mary, Phillip and Thomas. Based on this he writes that Jesus was married to Mary Magdalene and fathered a child. If this were so, why didn't Paul ever mention it? Paul had a golden opportunity when he defended his right to have a wife in I Corinthians 9:5-6. He mentions that Cephas (Peter), Barnabas, the other apostles and the brothers of the Lord all had wives. Had Jesus been married, Paul would certainly have brought it up here to clinch his argument.

Brown also states that nobody, even Jesus' followers, believed he was divine until Emperor Constantine declared Him the "Son of God" at the Council of Nicaea in A. D. 325. The four canonical Gospels, Paul's epistles and extra biblical testimony all indicate that Jesus was considered divine centuries before Nicaea. Moreover, a very early heresy in the life of the church (docetism) maintained that while Christ's deity was real and complete, His humanity was only appearance.

Each of the four canonical Gospels contains a reference to Mary Magdalene as a Galilean woman from whom seven demons were cast, who (with other women) viewed the

Crucifixion from a distance and who was the first to witness the Resurrection. Specifically, in Matthew 27:56, 61 and 28:1, we find, "Among which was Mary Magdalene, and Mary the mother of James and Joses, and the mother of Zebedee's children. . . And there was Mary Magdalene, and the other Mary, sitting over against the sepulcher. . . In the end of the Sabbath, as it began to dawn toward the first [day] of the week, came Mary Magdalene and the other Mary to see the sepulcher." Mark 15:40, 47, 16:1 and 9 tells us, "There were also women looking on afar off: among whom was Mary Magdalene, and Mary the mother of James the less and of Joses, and Salome; . . . And Mary Magdalene and Mary [the mother] of Joses beheld where he was laid. And when the sabbath was past, Mary Magdalene, and Mary the [mother] of James, and Salome, had bought sweet spices, that they might come and anoint him. . . Now when [Jesus] was risen early the first [day] of the week, he appeared first to Mary Magdalene, out of whom he had cast seven devils." Luke 8:2 and 24:10 states, "And certain women, which had been healed of evil spirits and infirmities, Mary called Magdalene, out of whom went seven devils, . . . It was Mary Magdalene, and Joanna, and Mary [the mother] of James, and other [women that were] with them, which told these things unto the apostles." Lastly, in John 19:25, 20:1 and 20:18 we read, "Now there stood by the cross of Jesus his mother, and his mother's sister, Mary the [wife] of Cleophas, and Mary Magdalene. . . The first [day] of the week cometh Mary Magdalene early, when it was yet dark, unto the sepulcher, and seeth the stone taken away from the sepulcher. . . Mary Magdalene came and told the disciples that she had seen the Lord, and [that] he had spoken these things unto her." Even if one reads in the apocryphal Gospels of Mary and Phillip that she kissed Jesus on the lips and that she debated a vision with Peter, it takes a tremendous leap of logic to conclude from just this that Jesus and Mary Magdalene were husband and wife.

Brown argues in his novel that a smear campaign by the early Church fathers distorted Mary Magdalene's role and effectively wrote her out of the official records. Professor Karen King of Harvard Divinity School states, "Mary got a raw deal." King and other feminist theologians erroneously conclude that the Church oppresses women, and thus attempts to make Mary Magdalene into something she was not in a further attempt to make the early Church what they wished it to be rather than what it was.

The Church is far from being an instrument of female oppression. A defining characteristic of Roman Catholicism has been the veneration of Mary, the Mother of God. This honor paid to Mary by them translates to an honor paid to all women because she is revered for uniquely fulfilling feminine roles. Even the pope submits to her authority.

Although to most Protestants, Mary unfortunately has become nothing more than a shadowy figure on a Christmas card, evangelical orthodox Protestants have always recognized her as a chosen vessel and the "Mother of our Lord." The early reformers also referred to her as the Mother of God. The Scriptures call her "Blessed." When Mary sung, under the inspiration of the Holy Spirit, the Magnificat, "My soul magnifies the Lord, and my soul has rejoiced in God my Savior" (Luke 1:46-7), she, at that moment, was putting her confidence and trust in the Child in her womb. Scripturally, we may conclude that Mary was the first Christian.

If the early Church fathers wanted to distort and down play the role of Mary Magdalene, and hence of women in the Church, why did they not eliminate the fact that she was the <u>first</u> to see our risen Lord and the <u>first to witness</u> to that fact to the disciples? These were major roles, and Christ assigned them to a woman, indeed to a fallen woman who had repented.

Because of the dubious association of the name of Mary Magdalene with the sinful woman in Luke 7, in England a reformed woman of ill fame was called a magdalen. There have been many religious communities (consisting of former prostitutes) named after Mary Magdalene. These communities are called Magdalenes and follow the Augustinian, Dominican and Franciscan rules. Although they are all extinct today, one convent still remains in Vilsbiburg.

So from Scripture and tradition that has been handed down by the early Church fathers, we have a woman, Mary Magdalene, who was healed of an infirmity by Jesus, who was one of His most faithful followers thereafter, who looked on when He was crucified, who saw Him buried, and who was the first to see Him after He arose from the dead. It seems to me if the intent of the early Church fathers was to downplay her and her role, and thereby distort the role of women in the Church, they did a very poor job of it.

Does the Roman Catholic Church provide a "loophole for the native on some distant island who may never have heard of Jesus?"

The specific term "Baptism by Desire" has not been used specifically in Catholic theology and therefore does not provides a "loophole" for the native on some distant island who may never have heard of Jesus. I think much of the confusion may come in making the proper distinctions between "a desire for Baptism" and what some refer to as "Baptism by desire." Nowhere to my knowledge does any Church council or even the current 1992 Catechism mention the term "Baptism by desire."

Catholic apologist Robert Sungenis states, "The only dogmatic place that this issue, (a desire for Baptism), is taught is at the Council of Trent, in three places. The first place is in session 6, chapter 4. Here, the Latin speaks more specifically to the individual's prior knowledge of baptism, and thus his 'desire' to fulfill his promise to receive baptism, rather than a 'baptism of desire.'"

This distinction can be seen in one of the other times that Trent uses the idea of "desire." The second place is in session 6, chapter 14:

> "Hence it must be taught that the repentance of a Christian after his fall is very different from that at his baptism, and that it includes not only a cessation from sins, and a detestation of them, or "a contrite and humble heart" (Psalm 50:1), but also the sacramental confession of the same, *at least in desire*, and to be made in its season, and sacerdotal absolution, as well as satisfaction by fasting, almsgiving, prayers, and other devout exercises of the spiritual life, not indeed for the eternal punishment, which is remitted together with the guilt either by the sacrament or the desire of the sacrament, but for the temporal punishment (Canon 3)], which (as the Sacred Writings teach) is not always wholly remitted, as is done in baptism . . ."

Here the individual (and this does not refer to some native on some distant island who never heard of Jesus) is understood as one who already knows of his responsibility to receive absolution in Confession for his sin, but perchance, doesn't live long enough to do so. In that case, the "desire" to fulfill his promise to go to Confession is sufficient. His "vow" to do so is reinforced by the other commitments he must honor, e.g., "as well as satisfaction by fasting, almsgiving, prayers, and other devout exercises of the spiritual life."

The 1992 Catechism also teaches the same. Paragraph 1258 states, "The Church has always held the firm conviction that those who suffer death for the sake of the faith without having received Baptism are baptized by their death for and with Christ. This Baptism of blood, like the desire for Baptism, brings about the fruits of Baptism without being a sacrament." Notice that the Catechism does not call it "baptism by desire," but "the desire for Baptism," which distinction acknowledges that the person fulfilling the category is one who already knows of his responsibility to receive baptism, and not some unknowing native.

This is also confirmed by the next paragraph of the Catechism (1259) which reiterates the Traditional interpretation of Trent's chapter 4 on the "desire for baptism," that is, that the desire for baptism applies in the first sense to catechumens. It states, "For catechumens who die before their Baptism, their explicit desire to receive it, together with repentance for their sins, and charity, assures them the salvation that they were not able to receive through the sacrament." The last time "desire" is mentioned at Trent is in Canon 4 on the Sacraments, "If anyone shall say that the sacraments of the New Law are not necessary for salvation, but are superfluous, and that, although all are not necessary for every individual, without them or without the desire of them through faith alone men obtain from God the grace of justification: let him be anathema."

Again, Trent, as does the Catechism, stresses the "desire for" the sacraments, NOT the "sacraments by desire." It is clearly stated that one who does not receive baptism or confession has not received the sacrament, even though they (consciously) "desired" the sacrament. The desire for the sacrament does not mean they have received the sacrament. They will be saved, according to Rome, without the sacrament if they (consciously) had a desire for the sacrament.

Theology is all about making the proper distinctions, and this is one of those times that proper distinctions must be made. All of the above is what has traditionally been taught of Baptism by the Roman Catholic Church and the desire for it, and is reiterated in the 1992 Catechism.

The speculative and non-resolved implications of desire for baptism as spelled out by Rome concern the issue of those who may have sought God in their lives (not those who supposedly never had any knowledge of Him), but had no knowledge of their responsibility to be baptized, or even knew of baptism. What is to be done for these kinds of people? The Roman Catholic Church has not given a definitive answer on this question, just as she has not given a definitive answer on the eternal destiny of an infant who dies without baptism. These issues are covered in paragraphs CCC 1260 and 1261 of the Catechism. As Pope Pius XI taught, "our knowledge concerning the recipients of salvation will take us only so far and no further, and to speculate beyond that point is not our prerogative."

Did Jesus know He would be crucified?

According to the Gospels, Jesus knew He would suffer crucifixion. Matthew 26:2 quotes Jesus as saying to His disciples, "You know that after two days the Passover is coming, and the Son of Man is to be delivered up for crucifixion." In John 12:32, Jesus says, "And I, if I be lifted up from the earth, will draw all men to Myself." In the next verse John explains, "But He was saying this to indicate the kind of death by which He was to die."

Even without assuming that Jesus had divine foreknowledge of the future, there is nothing improbable in the statement that He had a premonition not only that He would be put to death, but also that the method would be crucifixion. Under Roman law, that was the common mode of execution of persons condemned to death who were not Roman citizens. As Jesus traveled through Judea, Samaria and Galilee He must have often seen the bodies of the condemned hanging on crosses along the roads outside the gates of the towns and cities. He would naturally realize that if the authorities of

Jerusalem condemned Him to death the mode of execution would be crucifixion.

The Romans required the condemned to carry ones own cross to the place of execution. Cross, in the sense of meaning "burden" occurs in the Gospels several times previous to the crucifixion. Matthew 10:38 quotes Jesus saying, "And he who does not take his cross and follow after Me is not worthy of Me." In Luke 9:23 Jesus says, "If anyone wishes to come after Me, let him deny himself, and take up his cross daily, and follow Me." Some writers, assuming that the word "cross" did not acquire the meaning of a burden until after the crucifixion of Jesus, suppose these references to be anachronisms; that is, the authors of the Gospels ascribe to Jesus a figure of speech that would have been meaningless at the time He used it. That may be true, but it is not certain.

Why is Jesus called "The Man of Sorrows"?

Jesus is nowhere referred to as "The Man of Sorrows" in the New Testament. In fact the phrase itself does not occur anyplace in the entire New Testament.

It was suggested in the Old Testament by Isaiah 53:3, which reads "He was despised and forsaken of men, *a man of sorrows*, and acquainted with grief; And like one from whom men hid their face, He was despised, and we did not esteem Him." This part of the prophecy is interpreted as applicable to the Messiah and since the crucifixion; Christian writers have naturally applied it to Jesus.

Who was Barabbas?

Barabbas was a prisoner whom Pilate pardoned because the mob preferred his release to that of Jesus. *Bar*, equivalent to Aramaic *ben*, was a Chaldean loan-word meaning "son." *Barabbas* literally means "son of the father or master." In some manuscripts copies and ancient versions of Matthew, Barabbas first name is given as Jesus.

The Gospels say it was customary for the Roman governor to release at the Passover one prisoner whom the people desired. There is no other authority for this custom, which appears to have been comparable to birthday pardons granted by monarchs. Such an act of clemency would be appropriate to the Passover, a commemoration of the deliverance from bondage.

Barabbas was a notable prisoner. He was a robber, a murderer and one who was united with those bent on insurrection against Rome, making him popular with the zealots. Pilate was willing to release Jesus of Nazareth, but the chief priests and elders persuaded the multitude that they should ask for the release of Barabbas and the destruction of Jesus. So Pilate, willing to please the people released Barabbas and delivered Jesus to be crucified. Probably the two malefactors crucified with Jesus belonged to the rebels under Barabbas. The Gospels are silent on what became of Barabbas.

Who invented crucifixion?

The Romans did <u>not</u> invent crucifixion as a form of execution, as often stated. Crucifixion was probably of Oriental origin and was practiced by the ancient Assyrians, Persians, Egyptians, Phoenicians, Carthaginians and Greeks before it was by the Romans. Legend attributes the invention of crucifixion to Queen Semiramis of Assyria, who is reputed to have reigned at Babylon about 900 B.C. Herodotus cites numerous cases of crucifixion among the Persians and Greeks. He says that after Cyrus of Persia captured Babylon about 538 B.C. he crucified three thousand of the leading citizens as an example to the rest of the inhabitants. The Romans appear to have borrowed this form of capital punishment from the Greeks, who in turn had borrowed it from the Persians.

According to the Twelve Tablets, a code of Roman laws framed in the fifth century B.C., traitors were crucified in the Forum by being nailed to trees. After the suppression of the slave uprising led by Spartacus, the Thracian gladiator, six thousand of his followers were crucified in 71 B.C. on the high road between Capua and Rome.

The Jews were the victims of mass crucifixions after each one of several uprisings in Judea and Galilee from the time of Herod the Great until the last Jewish rebellion led by Bar Cochba in 132-135 A.D. Varus, governor of Syria when Jesus was a boy of ten or twelve, crucified two thousand Jews in Jerusalem after the suppression of a revolt. Josephus says that during the Jewish rebellion of 66 to 70 A.D., the Romans under Titus crucified so many Jews outside the walls of Jerusalem that "room was wanting for crosses, and crosses were wanting for bodies."

When did the Romans discontinue crucifixions?

Crucifixion continued to be the usual mode of executing slaves and malefactors in the Roman Empire until the fourth century A.D. Constantine the Great, emperor from 307 to 337 A.D., issued an edict abolishing crucifixions as a method of capital punishment. After that there were comparatively few executions by this method in Christendom. Although the cross had been previously used as an emblem by the Christians themselves, it was not until about this same time that it began to be used publicly as the generally acknowledged symbol of the Christian religion.

Constantine, the first Christian emperor of Rome, attached great importance to the cross. Legend says that he himself was converted to Christianity by a vision of a cross in the sky. The original cross on which Jesus was crucified was claimed to have been found by Constantine's mother, Helena, in Jerusalem. By Constantine's time the Christians were rapidly becoming the dominant religious group in the Empire and Rome had become cross conscious.

Who was Simon of Cyrene?

Other than what is in the Bible, we know nothing about Simon of Cyrene, whom the Roman soldiers compelled to carry the cross on which Jesus was crucified (Matthew 27:32 and Mark 15:21.) Simon of Cyrene was probably a Hellenistic Jew who resided at Cryene in Libya, in northern Africa. The Cyrenians were chiefly of Greek stock and were noted for their intellectual and business abilities.

From the Gospels we learn simply that Simon was a Cyrenian, that he was the father of Rufus and Alexander, that the mob met him coming in from the country soon after they left Pilate's judgment hall with Jesus on their way to the place of the execution, and they stopped the passerby and compelled him to carry the cross the remainder of the way. In Romans 16:13 Paul salutes "Rufus, a choice man in the Lord, also his mother" and it may be that this Rufus and his mother were the son and wife of Simon the Cyrene.

Some of the Gnostics of the early part of the Christian era taught the curious belief that Simon was mistakenly crucified in the place of Jesus. Upon their arrival at Golgotha, declared these Gnostics, Simon assumed the outward form of Jesus and Jesus assumed the outward form of Simon, which allowed Jesus to mingle with the crowd and escape. Other apocryphal writers related that it was Judas and not Simon the Cyrene who was thus substituted. Both of these speculations are totally unfounded and are not supported by Scripture.

Did the Jews crucify Jesus?

The Gospels clearly show that Jesus was "physically" crucified by the Romans on charges preferred and presented by the Jewish authorities in Jerusalem. In Palestine, crucifixion was a Roman and NOT a Jewish penalty which was stoning. The so-called Jewish council and the high priest were probably mere tools of Pilate and Rome.

John 18:31 says: "Pilate therefore said to them, "Take Him yourselves, and judge Him according to your law.' The Jews said to him, 'We are not permitted to put anyone to death.'" According to John 19:10, Pilate said to Jesus, "You do not speak to me? Do you not know that I have authority to release You, and I have authority to crucify You?"

The power of life and death had been taken away from the Jewish authorities and vested solely in the Roman procurator, who had authority to intervene in and to review all capital cases. It is clear in the Gospels that Jews initiated the action against Jesus, arrested Him, tried Him in the first instance and recommended the death penalty. Jesus was a Jew in nationality, race and religion and was so regarded by both the Roman and Jewish authorities.

Mark 10:33 quotes Jesus as saying, "Behold, we are going up to Jerusalem, and the Son of Man will be delivered up to the chief priests and scribes; and they will condemn Him to death, and will deliver Him up to the Gentiles." John 18:35 says, "Pilate answered, 'I am not a Jew am I? Your own nation and the chief priests delivered You up to me; what have You done?'"

Apparently, the Jewish authorities were interested in the charge that Jesus, in claiming to be the Messiah, had committed blasphemy, a purely religious offense. On the other hand, the Roman authorities were probably interested chiefly in the charge that Jesus, in claiming to be a king in the line of David, had committed treason, a purely political offense. The dual system of government caused the two charges to become confused.

We know from Luke 22:52, John 18:3 and John 18:12 that the arrest of Jesus was purely a Jewish action. Jesus' confession that He was the Messiah and the Son of God was regarded as sufficient evidence to convict Him of blasphemy. But Judaea was a Roman province and the Jewish authorities could not carry out the sentence. Luke 23:2 gives us the gist of the charges preferred by the Jewish authorities against Jesus before Pilate. When Pilate found no fault in the accused, the Jewish authorities pressed him further, and wishing to extricate himself from a difficult situation, sent Jesus to Herod Antipas, whose tetrarchy included Galilee and who happened to be in Jerusalem. This scheme did not work and Herod sent the prisoner back to Pilate. According to the Gospels, Pilate was willing to let Jesus off with a scourging, but the accusers demanded His crucifixion. This was too much for the vacillating Roman procurator, who apparently did not have the political courage to decide against the local authorities. Therefore, after washing his hands of the whole case, he said, "Take Him and crucify Him, I find no fault in Him."

This can hardly mean that Pilate expected the Jewish authorities themselves to crucify Jesus. Under the local Jewish law the witnesses in capital cases were also the legal executioners, and one might suppose that the order was directed to the Jewish rulers. But stoning, not crucifixion, was the Jewish method of execution, and the context makes it clear that Jesus was crucified by a detail of Roman soldiers commanded by a centurion.

Who these soldiers were, we have no means of knowing. Josephus says the Roman garrison in Judaea at the time was composed of Romans, Germans, Gauls, and Galatians. It was probably a mixed company that crucified Jesus in the Roman fashion. The title on the cross, JESUS KING OF THE JEWS, indicates that the Romans crucified Jesus on a charge of treason. The whole thing was a hasty affair, which took place at night and in the early part of the day and which involved trumped-up charges, false witnesses, political trickery and a confusion of Jewish and Roman procedures.

In later times it became customary among Christians to say that the Jews crucified Jesus. Much of the confusion and bitterness on this question arose from the fact that the New Testament uses *"Jew"* in several different senses. Since

Jesus and most of His early followers, as well as the authors of the New Testament, were Jews, obviously *"Jew"* in this connection refers to the Jewish authorities in Jerusalem and not the Jewish people. This distinction is generally made clear in the New Testament.

The Gospels themselves indicate that some members of the Jewish council in Jerusalem were friendly to Jesus. Both Nicodemus, who came to Jesus by night, and Joseph of Arimathea, who buried Jesus, were members of the Jewish council. When the early Jewish Christians accused "the Jews" of being responsible for the crucifixion of Jesus they meant the Jewish-Roman authorities in Jerusalem. For over fifteen hundred years Christians have been repeating in the Apostles' Creed, that Jesus "suffered under Pontius Pilate."

Christologically, it is all humanity who crucified Jesus. That is, theologically speaking, it is our (mankind's) fallen sin nature that was imputed (transferred) to Him and nailed Him to the cross.

Who were the two thieves crucified with Jesus?

The names of the two thieves crucified with Jesus are not given in the biblical accounts. Nothing whatever is known about these two "criminals" except what is written in the Four Gospels.

Matthew 27:38 calls the two "robbers." Luke 23 refers to them as "criminals," which emphasizes the fact that the Roman and Jewish authorities regarded Jesus as a common criminal. John 19:18 says, the two were crucified on either side of Jesus. Matthew 27:44 and Mark 15:32 imply that both thieves were impenitent at first. Only Luke tells about the penitent thief. John adds one more detail about the two thieves when he writes in 19:32 that the soldiers broke the legs of the two who were crucified with Jesus.

According to early Christian tradition, the name of the penitent thief was Dysmas. Roman Catholics regard him as a saint and his relics are claimed for Bologna, Italy. In some church calendars his feast day is commemorated March 25. The "good thief" is represented in art with a cross beside him. At the outskirts of the Judaean hills in Palestime is a village called Latrum. Originally the name was Natrun, but during the Middle Ages it was confused with the Latin *latro*, meaning robber, and from this circumstance grew up a legend that Latrun was the birthplace of the penitent thief. According to the apocryphal Gospel of Nicodemus, the impenitent thief crucified with Jesus was named Gestas.

Were the feet of Jesus nailed to the cross?

That the feet as well as the hands of Jesus were nailed to the cross is a popular presumption that is not supported by any passage in the New Testament. In art and literature Jesus is almost always represented as having been fastened to the cross by nails driven through both hands and feet.

The Four Gospels have little to say on this subject. Matthew and Mark mention neither hands nor feet in connection with the crucifixion. John tells us that one of the soldiers pierced the side of the body of the Savior after it was taken down. According to John 20:20, when Jesus appeared after His resurrection to some of His disciples, He showed them His hands and His side. Later in John 20:25 to 27, Jesus offered His hands and His side for Thomas to see and touch.

Luke does mention the feet of Jesus, but he says nothing to indicate that they were wounded. In Luke 24:39 Jesus does not call attention to His hands and His feet as wounded, but does so merely to identify Himself to His disciples that it is He with them in body and not in spirit.

Under the customary Roman method of crucifixion at that time the body of the victim was fastened to the cross by nails driven into the hands. Sometimes the feet were also nailed to the cross, but the more general practice was merely to bind them with cords. The idea that the feet of

Jesus were nailed to the cross was probably suggested by an Old Testament passage. In Psalms 22:16 we are told, "They pierced my hands and my feet." It is clear that the writers of the Gospels supposed this chapter to allude to the Messiah and consequently they connected it with Jesus as the Christ.

More than a dozen nails alleged to have been used in the crucifixion of Jesus are preserved as relics in different parts of the world. According to legend, Empress Helena, the mother of Constantine, found the nails used at the crucifixion at the same time and the same place where was discovered the true cross.

Another legend has it that the Empress once calmed the Adriatic during a terrific storm by throwing one of these nails into the sea. The finch known as the crossbill has sharply curved mandibles that cross each other, and a medieval story says Jesus bestowed these characteristics upon the bird because it attempted to release Him from the cross by trying to pull out the nails with its beak.

Did Judas hang himself or was he killed by a fall?

There are two accounts of the death of Judas in the Bible. Matthew 27:3-10 says that Judas went and hanged himself. Acts 1:18, however, says of Judas that he fell headlong, burst open in the middle and his bowels gushed out.

These two passages seem to present a serious discrepancy, which Bible scholars have attempted to reconcile with more ingenuity than success; although the explanation offered by Dr. D. James Kennedy of Coral Ridge Presbyterian Church in Florida, seems most reasonable. According to Dr. Kennedy, after Judas hanged himself, the rope broke or was cut and Judas fell headlong to the ground and burst asunder in the midst.

Other biblical scholars offer a less credible explanation by supposing that the author of Acts spoke only figuratively of Judas's end and did not intend to specify the actual manner of his death. Only one other biblical character committed suicide by hanging himself. In Samuel 17:23 we read that when Ahithophel's counsel was not followed, he packed up, went home, put his household in order, and hanged himself.

Why was Jesus offered vinegar at the crucifixion?

The purpose of the drink offered Jesus on the cross is not made clear by the Bible narratives. According to the Gospels, Jesus was offered drink twice. The Jews and the other by the Romans may have made one of these offers.

Mark 15:23 tells us that when Jesus was brought to Golgotha, they offered him wine mingled with myrrh, but He did not take it. Afterward, Jesus cried out with a loud voice (Mark 15:34-36) *Eloi, Eloi, lama sabachthani,* which translated is, My God, My God, why have you forsaken me? Then someone filled a sponge with vinegar, put it on a reed and gave it to Him to drink. Matthew 27:33-34 and 47-49 confirms the double offer of a drink but says that He tasted but did not drink the first time. The other two Gospels (Luke and John) say nothing about the first offer to drink. John 19:28-30 stated that these things were accomplished in order that the Scripture might be fulfilled, and that the sponge filled with vinegar was put upon hyssop. The Scriptural prophesy alluded to by John is apparently Palms 69:21. The hyssop in John appears to correspond with the reed in Matthew and Mark.

There seems to be no merit to the suggestion by some have that the hyssop was a spice added to the vinegar to make it quench thirst better. Just what the vinegar was and for what purpose it was offered to Jesus is not entirely clear.

There are three theories as to what the vinegar offered to Jesus was and as to why it was offered. One is that it was real vinegar and was offered to mock Him and further afflict Him. Another is that the drink consisted of a mixture of wine and myrrh such as kind and pious people were accustomed to offer a condemned person just before his execution to stupefy himself and to prevent unnecessary suffering. Still another is that those charged with His crucifixion merely wished to offer Him a drink out of kindness and sympathy.

From sources outside the Bible we learn that it was a custom among the Jews of that day to give a stupefying mixture of light wine and frankincense and myrrh to a person about to be executed to prevent unnecessary pain. This was undoubtedly the kind of drink first offered to Jesus before He was placed on the cross. The second drink offered to Jesus just before His death on the cross, was probably "posca" or sour wine ordinarily drunk by Roman soldiers. It was said that a drink of this sour wine was a privilege of any person who was crucified and thus the Roman soldiers would have had with them such a vessel of sour wine. It seems reasonable to suppose that the first drink was offered by Jews and the second by the Romans, and that some in each group made these customary acts out of mercy while others made it to mock Him.

When was the cross first used as a religious symbol?

The cross is among the oldest of all sacred symbols and there is evidence that it was used in various forms as a religious emblem by widely separated peoples long before the beginning of Christianity. Many centuries before the time of Jesus the ancient Egyptians venerated the cross and carved it on monuments and mummy cases, and put it on sacred cakes eaten as part of a religious ritual. In Egypt the cross may have acquired its sacred character because a cross-like device was used to measure the depth of the waters of the Nile.

The cross was a religious emblem among the Scandinavians, Druids, Etruscans, Sabines, Phrygians, Greeks, Romans and Hindus. The swastika, used as a mystic symbol among ancient Aryans, is a modified (indeed a twisted in more ways than one) cross. When Europeans first came to the New World they found the cross as an object of veneration among the Aztecs of

Mexico, the Incas of Peru and other Native American peoples. However, the cross as the emblem of Christianity originated with the crucifixion of Jesus and had no direct connection with its earlier use as a mystic and sacred symbol.

How many crucifixions are mentioned in the Bible?

Although crucifixions had been a common mode of execution in Palestine for centuries when the last books of the Bible were composed, it is an interesting fact that it contains no mention of any crucifixions except those of Jesus and the two malefactors crucified with Him. Crucifixion as a form of capital punishment was unknown to ancient Hebrew law.

A form of impaling after execution by stoning is referred to in Deuteronomy 21:22-23 which states in part that if a man commits a sin worthy of death and is put to death, he shall hang on a tree, but not into the night as he should be buried the same day. Joshua 10:26-27 tells that Joshua, after capturing the five kings in a cave, slew them and hanged them on five trees until evening. In Numbers 25:4, the Lord commanded Moses to take the heads of certain rebellious leaders and hang them in broad daylight. This obviously refers to the provision in the law that the body of any person so hanged was to be taken down and buried before sundown.

Josephus confirms certain New Testament passages relating to the crucifixion of Jesus when he says the Jews were so careful about burying the dead "that they took down those that were condemned and crucified, and buried them before the going down of the sun." These Old Testament references are not to crucifixion in the sense of nailing the condemned alive to a cross and leaving them there until death, but rather to a primitive form of posthumous indignity.

The Gentiles introduced crucifixions into Palestine at an early date. Josephus says Cyrus of Persia commanded that all persons who refused to help the Jews rebuild the temple at Jerusalem should be "caught and hung upon a cross."

King Demetrius of Syria, after capturing Jerusalem, crucified eight hundred Jews. Apparently some of the Maccabean Jewish kings imitated their Greek rivals in this respect, for Josephus tells us that Alexander Jannaeus, King of Judaea about 100 B.C., had eight hundred of his subjects crucified in Jerusalem.

Does the Bible call Jesus "The Prince of Peace"?

The phrase "Prince of Peace" occurs nowhere in the New Testament and only once in the Old Testament, in Isaiah 9:6, which is also sung in the "Halleluiah Chorus," Handle's Messiah. Christians regard this passage as a reference to the Messiah and therefore refer to Jesus as The Prince of Peace.

In the New Testament Jesus is several times referred to as a prince: "the Prince of life" in Acts 3:15, "a Prince and a Savior" in Acts 5:31, and "the prince of the kings of the earth" in Revelation 1:5. Over a period of twenty years beginning in 1904, William Jennings Bryan hundreds of times delivered his famous lecture entitled "The Prince of Peace," which did much to popularize the phrase in America.

Did Jesus have the power of making Himself invisible?

From a purely Christological view, of course He did since He was God. However, I suspect the questioner is referencing that biblical passage in Luke 4:30 where Jesus passed unseen through the multitude who sought to kill Him. That Jesus possessed and exercised the power of making Himself invisible to others is also faintly suggested in John 8:59.

I would read these passages as denoting nothing more that Jesus withdrew from the scene quietly and inconspicuously. Luke 24:31 tells us that immediately after the Resurrection, "He vanished from their sight." It is often stated that both Elijah and Elisha had the power of making themselves invisible or partially so, but this is not borne out by any passage in the Bible.

Was Judas treasurer of Jesus and His disciples?

The popular notion that Judas Iscariot acted as treasurer or steward for Jesus and His disciples rests on two passages in the New Testament. John 12:4-6, in connection with Mary's anointing the feet of Jesus with a costly ointment says, "But Judas Iscariot, one of His disciples, who was intending to betray Him, said ' Why was this ointment not sold for three hundred denari, and given to poor people?' Now he said this, not because he was concerned about the poor, but because he was a thief, and as he had the money box, he used to pilfer what was put into it."

At the Last Supper Jesus dipped a morsel and gave it to Judas saying, "What you do, do quickly." John 13:28-29 says, "Now no one of those reclining at table knew for what purpose He had said this to him. For some were supposing, because Judas had the money box, that Jesus was saying to him, 'Buy the things we have need of for the feast'; or else, that he should give something to the poor." Matthew, Mark and Luke make no illusion to the fact that Judas acted as treasurer and steward for Jesus and His disciples.

When did Jesus ask His disciples to arm themselves?

According to Luke 22:36 Jesus at the last supper said to the Twelve Apostles, "let him who has no sword sell his robe and buy one." Previously Jesus had spoken of the sword in the symbolic sense. In Matthew 10:34 He is quoted as saying, "Do not think that I came to bring peace on earth; I did not come to bring peace, but a sword." Luke 22:38 adds, "And they said, 'Lord, look, here are two swords.' And He said to them, 'It is enough.'"

Those who argue for a literal interpretation presume it was with one of the swords that Peter cut off the right ear of the servant of the high priest in the garden of Gethsemane on the night that Jesus was arrested. (See Matthew 26:51-54, Mark 14:46-47, Luke 22:49-51 and John 18:10-11; only John 18:10-

11, supplies the names of persons who cut off the servant's ear, Simon Peter, as well as that of the servant, Malchus.) Only Luke mentions that Jesus healed the servant's ear.

This sword incident is one of the most difficult in the New Testament to explain. It is hard to believe that Luke 22:38 means literally that Jesus asked His little band of disciples to arm themselves with a view to resisting the authorities. Such a conclusion seems to be inconsistent with the words and spirit of the rest of the Gospels. In Revelation 13:10 we are told, "If anyone kills with the sword, with the sword he must be killed."

I personally have read Luke 22:38 symbolically to mean the Old and the New Testaments. Ephesians 6:17 defines the Word of God (the Bible) as a sword, and in Revelation 22:18, Jesus warns against adding to Scripture. Consequently, when Jesus states that the two swords that the apostles present in Luke 22:38 "are enough", I interpret it to mean He is referring to the Old and the New Testaments as being "enough" to fully present the Word of God to the world.

Why was doubting Thomas also called Didymus?

The term doubting Thomas, meaning one who will not believe until he sees, an incredulous person or a habitual doubter, is not in the Bible, but was suggested by the fact that the apostle Thomas refused to believe in the resurrection of Jesus until he had seen with his own eyes. This incident is related only in the Gospel of John, in chapter 20 verses 24 through 29. Because of this passage this Apostle has come down through the centuries as Doubting Thomas, the typical pessimist and skeptic. On at least one other occasion Thomas is a doubter. According to John 14:4-5, after Jesus has said, "And you know the way where I am going," Thomas said to Jesus, "Lord, we do not know where You are going: how do we know the way?"

In the gospels of Matthew, Mark and Luke he is simply called Thomas, but in John he is referred to as "Thomas, called Didymus." Didymus is merely a literal Greek translation of the Aramaic form of Thomas and signifies "twin." Some authorities suppose Didymus alluded to his doubting propensities and in some versions it is translated "double minded." Others, however, suppose Didymus was originally an editor's note to explain the meaning of the name. Since the names of Thomas and Matthew are linked together in the lists of the Twelve Apostles in Matthew, Mark and Luke, one theory is that they may have been twin brothers, but in Acts 1:13 Thomas's name is separated from that of Matthew by Bartholomew.

What is Maundy Thursday?

Maundy Thursday is the name given to the Thursday of Holy Week, the week between Palm Sunday and Easter, and is the day in which the Last Supper was instituted as Jesus and His disciples celebrated Passover. The word "Maundy" is derived but corrupted from "mandatum," the first word of the rite of washing of feet. This act, retained in the Roman Catholic liturgy of Holy Thursday, is one of humble example, for it was a lesson in humility that Christ performed this service of washing His disciples feet. This story is recorded in John 13:1-17. This act can also be one of symbolizing purification.

What was the value of the betrayal money?

It is impossible to determine in terms of modern money the exact value of the thirty pieces of silver that Judas received for betraying Jesus. The Hebrew equivalent of piece of silver appears to have been applied at various times to different coins and weights of monetary metal. In the time of Jesus it probably was merely a popular name for the most common silver coin in circulation. Exodus 21:32 says, "If the ox gores a male or female slave, the owner shall give his or her master thirty shekels of silver, and the ox shall be stoned."

One authority says that the value of a piece of silver was one sum in the Pentateuch (the first five books of the Old Testament), another in the books of the prophets and still another in other Old Testament writings. Matthew, the only Gospel to refer to the price of betrayal as thirty pieces of silver, in chapter 27 verse 9 relates the actual amount to a prophecy in Zechariah 11:12,13.

If a piece of silver was the prevalent coin of the time, the money received by Judas was probably thirty Tyrian shekels, which were the customary temple offerings and which were worth about fifty cents a piece in US currency. If this is true, Judas betrayed his Master for about fifteen dollars. Some have supposed it must have been a larger sum, because after Judas returned the money the priests used it to purchase potter's field. This, however, is not conclusive, because we have no means of knowing what the potter's field was or what it was worth. It may have been a comparatively worthless piece of property. Some have suggested that is was a riverbed where potters mined for clay. There simply is not sufficient information on the subject to form a conclusion. Thirty pieces of silver has become the proverbial name for a bribe or blood money.

What did the robe worn by Jesus look like?

The garment worn by Jesus is frequently mentioned in the Gospels but never specifically described. It may be assumed that Jesus wore the customary Jewish dress of the time. This probably consisted of a kerchief to cover the head, coarse linen undergarments, a long loose outer garment variously called a coat, cloak, mantle or robe, a leathern girdle and sandals. On special ceremonial or dress occasions, Jewish men wore a loose robe with short sleeves in place of the usual girdled robe. It was probably such a robe that Jesus laid aside when He washed the feet of His disciples after the Last Supper as recorded in John 13:4.

That Jesus wore the regulation Jewish costume is indicated by references to the hem of His garment that, when touched, made people whole, as recorded in Matthew 9:20-22 and in Matthew 14:34-36. Hem in these passages should really be rendered borders or tassels. In Numbers 15:38 and 39 Jews were commanded to make tassels for the corners of their garments to look at to remember all the commandments of the Lord, and to do them. Nothing was more natural for Jews who believed in the miraculous powers of Jesus to seek to touch that part of His garment that they regarded as most holy.

Was the color of Jesus' robe scarlet as Mark tells us, or purple as Matthew and John tell us, or is there a contradiction in Scripture?

In Matthew 27:28-31 we are told that the soldiers, after Pilate had delivered Jesus to them to be crucified, stripped Him and put on Him a scarlet robe. But after they mocked and ill-treated Him as pretender to the throne of Israel, they took that robe off Him and put His own garments back on Him. Mark 15:17 says they clothed Him in "purple" (really a term for shades varying from rose to purple, thus there is no real contradiction to the account in Matthew) and afterwards put His own clothes back on Him. John 19:2 uses that same term "purple" to describe the color of the robe. A scarlet or "purple" robe was the emblem of royalty and therefore appropriate for their mockery of one whom they charged had "pretended to be King of the Jews."

Was Jesus clothed when He was crucified?

Although artists frequently depict Jesus barely clothed, the above passages (Matthew 27:28-31, Mark 15:17 and John 19:2) indicate that Jesus was wearing His usual clothes when He was crucified. Matthew 27:35 says, "And when they had crucified Him, they divided up His garments among themselves, casting lots." This was a clear fulfillment of the Messianic prophesy as recorded by David in Psalms 22:18, "They divided my garment among them, and for my clothing they cast lots." Luke 23:34 also records the fulfillment of this prophecy while John 19:23 and 24 gives the most detailed account of the incident. In those days the garments of the condemned were the perquisites of the executioners. John's passage indicates that there were four soldiers in immediate charge of the crucifixion of Jesus.

What became of the robe worn by Jesus?

Nothing whatever is known of the fate of Jesus' garments. What became of the seamless coat of Jesus for which the soldiers cast lots is the theme of The Robe, a novel by Lloyd Douglas, published in 1942 and of "Robe of Calvary" an inspirational hit song released in 1954.

What was the name of Pontius Pilate's wife?

There is only one direct reference to the wife of Pontius Pilate in the New Testament and that does not give her name. In connection with the trial of Jesus before the Roman procurator, Matthew 27:19 tells us that Pilate's wife said to him, "Have nothing to do with that righteous Man; for last night I suffered greatly in a dream because of Him." History is equally silent on the name of Pilate's wife. Later Christian tradition gives her the name of Claudia, Procula, or Procla and says that she was inclined toward Judaism if not actually a Jewish proselyte and a secret follower of Jesus.

Some authorities, with little justification have identified Pilate's wife with the Claudia mentioned by Paul in II Timothy 4:21. This Claudia was probably a Roman Christian. In Christian tradition she is regarded as a relative of either Pudens or of Linus, who became Bishop of Rome and is listed second, next to Peter, among the Popes. On the strength of the tradition that Pilate's wife was a secret follower of Jesus and that her name was Claudia the Greek Orthodox Church canonized her as a saint, and her feast day is October 27.

Why are criminals executed on Friday?

The early custom of executing criminals on Friday, which in Europe dates back at least to the Middle Ages, is supposed by some authorities to have arisen from the fact that Jesus was executed by crucifixion on Friday, the sixth day of the week according to the old Jewish calendar. Although the practice is not so prevalent as formerly, no adequate explanation has ever been offered as to why the sixth day of the week should have been preferred as the day for executions.

It is generally assumed, with some reason, that the ill luck associated with Friday by superstitious people arose form the connection of that day with the crucifixion of Jesus: but the assertion that the old practice of setting that day for executions resulted from this belief is mere speculation. Friday was popularly known as hangman's day. Whether the superstition associated with Friday was suggested by the fact that it was hangman's day, or whether condemned criminals were put to death on that day because of the ill luck associated with it, we have no means of determining. Curiously enough, the ancient Scandinavians, as well as the Hindus, regarded Friday as the luckiest day of the week.

Does the Bible mention Easter?

Easter occurs once in the King James Version of the Bible, but not in its present sense. Acts 12:4 tells us that Herod, after arresting Peter and delivering him to the soldiers, intended "after Easter to bring him forth to the people." Here Easter refers to the Passover and it is so rendered in other versions.

Easter is supposed to be derived from Anglo-Saxon "Eostre," the name of a Norse goddess whose festival was celebrated by the pagans at the vernal equinox. the root of the term probably signified rising or rebirth and Ester was the pagan festival to welcome the return of spring, a season of new birth and growth. The Anglo-Saxons called April "easter month" because it was the month in their clime when the buds began to open. In the course of time Easter became the English name for the festival commemorating the resurrection of Jesus. It is to the Christians (in part) what the Passover is to the Jews and what the spring was to the pagans.

How did *Passover* originate?

Moses ordained the Passover before the Israelites left Egypt more than three thousand years ago, and this feast has been observed continuously longer than any elaborate religious rite. The entire first born in Egypt were condemned to die in the last of the ten plagues. Moses told each family of Israelites to kill a lamb and sprinkle the blood on their posts and remain in their homes until they received orders to leave Egypt.

Exodus 12:23 says, "For the Lord will pass through to strike the Egyptians; and when He sees the blood on the lintel and on the two doorposts, the Lord will pass over the door and not allow the destroyer to come into your houses to strike you." *Pass over* in this text is only a rough English equivalent of the Hebrew original. The Hebrew *pasach*, translated *pass over* in English, signified "to protect," "to deliver" or "to pass by, or to pass over, in the sense of to spare."

The application of *pasach* to the sacrificial lamb killed and eaten at this feast may have been influenced by the fact that the Assyrian *pasahu* meant, "to propitiate." The English translators in turn may have been influenced by the fact that Anglo-Saxon *opher* meant "a sacrifice," or "victim" and *pasch-opher* meant "paschal offering."

Moses commanded the Israelites to observe the Passover forever to commemorate their exodus from Egyptian bondage. This seven-day festival begins on the fourteenth day of the first month of the Hebrew calendar and lasts until the twenty-first day.

Why is unleavened bread used in the Passover?

Leavened bread is the symbol of ceremonial pollution and unclearness, and the eating of unleavened bread during the Passover and the feast of the unleavened bread was suggested by the fact that the Israelites left Egypt in such haste that they had no time to leaven their bread. Some authorities suppose the Passover and the feast of unleavened bread were originally separate feasts and that they were later fused into one; but it seems more probable that the feast of unleavened bread was at first one ceremonial event during the feast of seven days now known as Passover.

What is the significance of the Passover lamb?

Mosaic law prescribed that the Passover lamb be a male yearling without blemish, roasted whole and eaten at one meal. It was eaten as a peace offering, its blood was sprinkled as in the ritual of atonement, and the remains were consumed as in burnt offerings.

How does the Eucharist or the Lord's Supper relate to the Passover?

To fully understand the new covenant sacrament of the Eucharist, it must be understood in the context of its old covenant types and shadows. The New Testament account of the institution of the Lord's Supper presupposes a basic understanding of the old covenant types and shadows.

Jesus instituted the Lord's Supper in the context of the Jewish Passover. There are some questions among New Testament scholars regarding the precise chronology of the Last Supper, but there is no doubt that the authors of the Gospels placed the institution of the Last Supper in the general context of the Passover. In the twelfth chapter of the book of Exodus God outlines the various elements of the Passover observance.

First, the Passover was a communal act of worship with a particular emphasis on families. Second, the blood of the Passover lamb is a sign distinguishing the people of God from those outside the covenant. A covenant is a bond in blood. Sacrificial blood is necessary for both cleansing and sanctification and Jesus fulfilled this completely and perfectly in His sacrifice of Himself. The blood distinguished the covenant people of God from those outside the covenant and it averted the judgment of God. Third, the Passover involves a sacrifice and a sacrificial meal. The slaying of the lamb is the sacrifice proper; the eating of the lamb is the sacrificial meal in which those who eat are made partakers of the sacrifice; it was a common way of sealing of the covenant. Jesus referred to His own blood as the blood of the covenant and inaugurated a new phase in the history of redemption.

Fourth, the observance of the Passover is a memorial feast in which the mighty act of God in redemption is remembered. In Jesus we have the final, once for all sacrifice symbolized by all of the old covenant sacrifices. Jesus is the true bread from heaven that God has provided to fulfill our spiritual need. Fifth, the future generations who observe the Passover will remember this past act of God but also have a dramatic reenactment of this decisive act of redemption. Just as the worshipper in Israel was required to partake of the old covenant peace offering, today's worshipper is commanded to partake of the new covenant peace offering.

In the ancient Passover there was no dessert or after dish, yet it was after the Passover meal that Jesus added a new dish. He instituted a new memorial by the breaking of the bread. Later, after the destruction of the Temple in A. D. 70 a new after dish was added to the Passover meal. It is called the *aphikomen*, a wafer of unleavened bread. The word *aphikomen* comes from the Greek word *epikomios* meaning "that which comes last."

During the Passover meal, the host takes the *aphikomen*, breaks it in half, puts one half between two pieces of unleavened bread, wraps the remaining half in a white napkin or white silk bag and hides of buries it. The children will search for the hidden *aphikomen* and the child who finds it, turns it over to the host who gives the child a small gift, usually a small sum of money. The host unwraps the *aphikomen* and distributes olive sized pieces to everyone. By rabbinic tradition, an olive-sized morsel is the smallest over which a blessing may be said. Eating the *aphikomen* officially concludes the meal.

One may readily make several Christian analogies from the observance described above. The three pieces of unleavened bread depict the triune nature of God with the middle wafer, the *aphikomen* that is broken and buried, representing Christ.

The Lord's Supper is a ceremony that seals and ratifies a covenant. It is an offering of thanksgiving, a Eucharist celebrated by Gentiles across the world. In its observance we proclaim the greatness of the name of our Lord Jesus Christ.

What is the significance of Passover for Christians?

The Last Supper eaten together by Jesus and His disciples was in observance of Passover. Matthew 26:17 says, "Now on the first day of the Feast of the Unleavened Bread the disciples came to Jesus, saying to Him, 'Where do You want us to prepare for You to eat the Passover?'" We are told that the disciples did as Jesus instructed them, they made ready the Passover and when evening came, Jesus sat down with the twelve. For Christians, the death of Jesus became symbolical of the killing of the sacrificial lamb at the Passover. In First Corinthians 5:7 Paul says, "Therefore purge out the old leaven, that you may be a new lump, since you truly are unleavened. For indeed Christ, our Passover, was sacrificed for us." In the course of time the Hebrew *pasach*, Passover, became Latin *pascha*, Easter.

Can you tell me where, in the Bible, I can find the story of the woman who wipes Jesus' face after He stumbles while carrying His cross as depicted in the movie, "The Passion Of The Christ."

That story, commonly known as "Veronica's Veil," is not in the Bible. Rather, according to legend, a Jewish woman is said to have wiped Jesus' bleeding and perspiring face with her veil upon which His image was imprinted forever.

According to The Catholic Dictionary, (p. 160) "this likeness was brought to Rome in 700, and it belongs this day to the relics of St. Peter's church at Rome, where it is only shown to persons of princely rank, who, however, first must be made titular canons of St. Peter's." The dictionary goes on to explain that Veronica, came by error, to be the name of a person as the word "veronica" was a compound of *vera* and *icon*, meaning "true image," and that the name Veronica was initially given to the image itself and not to the woman. Although Veronica is not included among the official listing of saints, her feast day is July 12.

In the movie, "The Passion Of The Christ," why is Mary Magdalene connected with the unnamed woman taken in adultery?

There is no biblical evidence that supports the idea that Mary Magdalene was an adulterer or a prostitute. Mary Magdalene is mentioned very few times in the Bible. The only things written about her are: Christ cast seven demons from her; she witnessed the crucifixion from afar; she watched Christ's burial; she was with the group of women who went to sepulcher early upon the first day of the week with spices and ointments; and she was the first person to whom the risen Lord manifested Himself.

The leading theory is that Pope Gregory intentionally changed her identity, perhaps reflecting what was already popular opinion. The person of Mary Magdalene was combined with the anonymous sinner in Luke who anointed Jesus' feet. With that in mind, it is often assumed that the "forgiven sinner" who anointed Jesus' feet was a prostitute, and the connection is made. From this, plus the statement that Jesus had cast seven demons out of her (Luke 8:2), has risen the tradition that she had been a prostitute before she met Jesus. There are those who continue to hold the prostitute view regardless of her actual status as such because of the centuries invested in that particular legend. Nevertheless she has come to be a symbol for not only penitence and redemption, but also of sexuality and female strength.

Do Moslems believe in the Bible?

Mohammed based his teachings largely upon the Old and New Testaments, upon Arabic tradition and upon his own philosophy. It is generally supposed that Mohammed obtained his knowledge of the Scriptures orally by conversing with Arabic Jews and Christians rather than from reading the Bible. The Bible plays a very minor role in Islam. Moslem authorities hold that wherever the Koran differs from the Bible, the Jews and Christians have corrupted or perverted the Biblical text.

Moslems recognize six prophets: Adam, Noah, Abraham, Moses, Jesus and Mohammed. Mohammed regarded himself as the successor of Jesus and the last of the prophets. Of the other five prophets of Islam, Abraham and Jesus are regarded as the principal ones. Islam, like Judaism, is a strictly monotheistic religion, and Moslems do not worship Mohammed or any of the other prophets as a deity. The essence of Islam is, "There is only one God, Allah, and Mohammed is his prophet." Consequently, the Moslems, while they accept Jesus as one of the six prophets, do not worship Him or hold to a triune God as Christians do. Moslems, like the Gnostics (erroneously in my personal opinion), believe that Jesus was not Himself crucified but another in His likeness.

How many chapters and verses does the King James Version of the Bible contain?

The King James Version of the Bible contains 1,189 chapters, 929 of which are in the Old Testament and 260 in the New Testament. Psalm 117, the shortest chapter in the Bible, is also the middle chapter, being preceded by 594 and followed by the same number.

There are 23,214 verses in the Old Testament and 7,959 in the New Testament, for a total of 31,173 in the Bible. Psalm 18:8 is the middle verse.

How many angels are referred to by name in the Bible?

Only two angels are mentioned by name in the Protestant Bible. They are Gabriel and Michael. In Daniel 8:16 Gabriel is the name of the revealing angel who appeared to Daniel in a dream to interpret his vision, although angel is not used in that particular connection. In Daniel 9:21 we read, "Yea, while I was speaking in prayer, even the man Gabriel, whom I had seen in the vision at the beginning, being caused to fly swiftly, touched me about the time of the evening oblation."

Gabriel is not again referred to by name until Luke 1, where we are told that an angel of the Lord appeared to Zacharias while he executed the priest's office and burned incense in the temple. After the angel had foretold that the priest's wife Elizabeth should bear him a son, whose name should be called John, Zacharias asked, "Whereby shall I know this?" According to Luke 1:19, the angel answered, "I am Gabriel, who stands in the presence of God, and I am sent to speak to you, and to show you these glad tidings."

Later Gabriel also appears to Mary in Luke 1:26-27, "And in the sixth month the angel Gabriel was sent from God."

Michael is not called an angel in Daniel, but is mentioned in Daniel 10:13 and again in verse 21 as a chief prince. Michael reappears in Jude in verse 9 (which book is too short to be divided into chapters) where it says Michael, the archangel contended with the devil. In Revelation 12:7-8 we read of the war in heaven in which Michael and his angels fought against the dragon.

Lucifer, popularly regarded as a fallen angel, occurs in the Bible only once. Isaiah 14:12 says, "How art thou fallen from heaven, O Lucifer, son of the morning; how art thou cut down to the ground, which didst weaken the nations!" But Lucifer, Satan and the Devil, under various names, are referred to in the Bible as commanding angels rather than being angels themselves. Revelation 12:9 says, "And the great dragon was cast out, that old serpent, called the Devil, and Satan, which deceives the whole world: he was cast out into the earth, and his angels were cast out with him." The Hebrew word translated Lucifer signifies "day star,' while that translated Satan means "adversary."

Two additional angels are mentioned by name in the Catholic Bible, in the Old Testament Apocrypha. Tobias 12:14 refers to Raphael as one of seven angels who present the prayers of the saints, while Uriel is the angel who appears to Ezra in II Esdras 4:1. The ancient Hebrews did not think of angels as individual entities with names, but merely as the messengers of God.

Does the Bible say that angels have wings?

Nowhere in the King James Version of the New Testament are angels spoken of as having wings, although in his vision on Patmos, according to Revelation 8:13 and 14:6, John heard an angel flying. The popular notion that faithful Christians after death are transformed into angels with two wings is hardly justified by any passage in the Bible.

Isaiah describes seraphim with six wings each (Isaiah 6:12), and the cherubim that Ezekiel saw had four wings (Ezekiel 1:11). In his vision Zechariah saw two women, with wind in their wings, "for they had wings like the wings of a stork" (Zechariah 5:9). The cherubs of gold at the ends of the Mercy Seat on the Ark of the Covenant (Exodus 25:20) had two wings each. These latter references to images of cherubs, and the reference in Zechariah, appear to be the only instances in which angels of any order are referred to in the Bible as two winged creatures.

Some authorities suppose that the Hebrew borrowed their conception of winged seraphim and cherubim from the Assyrians and Persians, who depicted winged men with heads of hawks on the walls of their buildings, and whose palaces were guarded by sculptured winged bulls and lions. Both the Greek word from which angel is derived, and the Hebrew word so translated in the Bible, signify "messenger." In the Old Testament angels were the messengers of God. In the New Testament Jesus is substituted for the angels as the intermediary between God and man.

What was the function of a prophet?

It is a common mistake to suppose that the sole function of the prophets in ancient Israel was to foretell the future. Prophet is from a Greek word meaning "to announce" or to "forth-tell" and that was the general significance of the Hebrew words rendered prophet in the Old Testament.

Originally the prophets were men and women who established themselves in the theocracy as spiritual leaders, preachers, orators, writer, poets, teachers, priests, and statesmen. Prophesying in the later sense of the term was only incidental to their general functions. It was the later apocalyptical prophets who cause the word to be associated mainly with future sayings rather than with practical matters.

Abraham, Isaac, Jacob, Moses, Aaron, Miriam and other early civil and spiritual leaders are all referred to as prophets and prophetesses. Deborah, for instance, did not foretell the future but was called a prophetess because she was inspired to direct the Israelites in a crisis.

The prophets were the inspired spokesmen of the Lord. In Deuteronomy 18:20-22 Moses himself laid down a rule for judging true and false prophets: "But the prophet who presumes to speak a word in My name, which I have not commanded him to speak, or who speaks in the name of other gods, that prophet shall die. And if you say in your heart, 'How shall we know the word which the Lord has not spoken?' When a prophet speaks in the name of the Lord, if the thing does not happen or come to pass, that is the thing which the Lord has not spoken; the prophet has spoken it presumptuously; you shall not be afraid of him."

Jesus, who like John the Baptist, was called a prophet, laid down a similar rule. According to Matthew 7:15-16 Jesus said in the Sermon on the Mount: "Beware of false prophets, who come to you in sheep's clothing, but inwardly they are ravenous wolves. You will know them by their fruits. Do men gather grapes from thorn bushes or figs from thistles?"

Some of the writing prophets were literary men of great power and energy. With every serious crisis in ancient Israel there emerged one great prophet or more to speak the words of the Lord to both the rulers and the people. Established prophets were privileged persons. They were permitted to enter even the palace and to state their messages from heaven into the ears of the king on his throne.

I Samuel 9:9 says: "Formerly in Israel, when a man went to inquire of God, he spoke thus: 'Come, let us go to the seer;' for he who is now called a prophet was formerly called a seer." This suggests some sort of change in the function of prophets was taking place during the time of Samuel. Apparently, however, seer and prophet have become transposed in this passage because seer is never once used before, while prophet is used often in the earlier books of the Old Testament. A seer was one who could see past, present or future things that were hidden or secret to others.

Through one of his prophets, according to Joel 2:28, the Lord said in the time to come that He, "will pour out My Spirit on all flesh; Your sons and your daughters shall prophesy, Your old men shall dream dreams, Your young men shall see visions."

How many prophetesses are mentioned in the Bible?

Prophetess is applied to five persons in the Bible in the sense of women who exercised the function of a prophet. Four of these are in the Old Testament and one in the New.

The first is in Exodus 15:20 where Miriam, the sister of Moses and Aaron is referred to as a prophetess. The second is in Judges 4:4 where Deborah, the wife of Lapidoth and the one who judged Israel at that time, is called a prophetess. She inspired Barak and helped him plan the campaign that ended in the defeat of the Canaanites at the battle of Kishon. This victory is the subject of "The Song of Deborah" found in Judges 5. The third prophetess mentioned in the Bible is Huldah who, according to II Kings 22:14 dwelt in the college in Jerusalem, the college with whom Hilkiah and his associates communed. The fourth Old Testament prophetess, Noadiah, is mentioned in Nehemiah 6:14 which says: "My God, remember Tobiah and Sanballat, according to these their works, and the prophetess Noadiah and the rest of the prophets who would have made me afraid."

We read about Anna, the only New Testament prophetess in Luke 2:36-37, "Now there was one, Anna, a prophetess, the daughter of Phanuel, of the tribe of Asher. She was of a great age, and had lived with a husband seven years from her virginity; and this woman was a widow of about eighty-four years, who did not depart from the temple, but served God with fastings and prayers night and day.

Isaiah 8:3 uses prophetess in the simple sense of the wife of a prophet. Likewise, in the Islamic faith, Aveshah, the second wife of Mohammed, is known as a prophetess. Since Mohammed is the Prophet of Islam, his most beloved wife is spoken of as the Prophetess or Madame Prophet.

Prophetess is employed in a figurative sense in Revelation 2:20, "Nevertheless I have a few things against you, because you allow that woman Jezebel, who calls herself a prophetess, to teach and seduce My servants to commit sexual immorality and eat things sacrificed to idols." In Acts 21:9 we are told this about Philip the evangelist, whom Paul visited at Caesarea, "Now this man had four virgin daughters who prophesied," but these women are not specifically referred to as prophetesses.

Who composed the Apostles' Creed?

The religious formula known as the Apostles' Creed is one of the most ancient and widely accepted rules of Christian faith and was so called either because its composition was traditionally ascribed to the Twelve Apostles themselves or because it was regarded as an epitome of their teachings. In 108 simple words it contains all the essential elements of the Christian faith in twelve statements or articles. When, where, why, by whom and in what language it was originally composed are matters merely for speculation rather than positive proof.

According to a legend that seems to date back only to the Middle Ages the creed was written on the day of Pentecost and each Apostle contributed one article. This, of course, was after Matthias had been chosen (see Acts 1:26) to fill the vacancy among the twelve caused by the desertion and suicide of Judas. Whether or not the Apostles authorized the creed, its substance was derived from the Gospels and the other Apostolic writings. It may have been suggested by Peter's great confession in Mathew 16:16, when he said, "You are the Christ, the Son of the living God." A somewhat similar formula existed in Greek in the second century. It is mentioned by St. Irenaeus, who died in 202 AD.

What is meant by the quick and the dead?

Quick is derived from Anglo-Saxon *cwic*, meaning "living" or "animate." The quick and the dead are the living and the dead. In this sense "quick" is now regarded as archaic or dialectical, except in the phrase under consideration. We find the phrase used in the King James Version in Acts 10:42 and in Second Timothy 4:1 and in the original form of the Apostles' Creed.

Shakespeare has Hamlet tell the clown that the grave "is for the dead, not for the quick," and later the Prince of Denmark says to Laertes, "Be buried quick with her, and so will I," which means, "Be buried alive with her" and not "Be buried at once with her." Quick in such words as quicksand, quicklime and quicksilver retains a degree of this earlier meaning of the term.

Why do you think people join churches?

The majority of church members today do not know what are the fundamental tenants of their church, nor do they know why they are members of a particular denomination. Most cannot give sufficient biblical or theological reasons why they are members of a particular denomination as opposed to being a member of another denomination or even for being a member of a non-denominational church. There is a great need for church members to know clearly what they believe and why.

It is my opinion that when people join churches they are guided by feeling rather than by judgment. People do not first ascertain the leading principles of the denomination or of an independent church from its acknowledged standards, and then examine these principles in the light of the Word of God. Most people do not take the time to search for principles and weigh them but rather are influenced in their choice, either by the authority of some great men, or the moral worth of some particular persons, or the piety and eloquence of some local minister, or by how comfortable they are with the order and style of worship.

It matters not that within denominations and non-denominational churches there are some that deny the deity of Jesus Christ, His virgin birth, His personal and visible return, the inerrancy of Scripture, etc. Instead of realizing that there is such a polarization of theological beliefs most people today are attracted to "feel good" worship services. The sad thing about that is that worship is not for us, but for God.

What does a "creedal and confessional" church mean?

First, it should be noted that there are slight differences between creeds and confessions. It could be said that creeds such as the three classic creeds (Apostles', Nicene and Athanasian) seek to enumerate the unifying essentials of the church universal for all ages. A creed deals with the fundamentals of the church. A confession, on the other hand, is a more detailed treatment of theology.

Creedal and confessional churches would affirm that the statements set forth in the ancient creed and its particular confessions are accurate statements of Scriptural Truth, as far as fallible men can discern. They would say that the creeds and their confessions contain the system of doctrine as taught in the Bible.

In saying this, creedal and confessional churches do not place the creeds and confessions on par with the Bible. Creeds and confessions are not independent assertions of truth serving as supplemental material to Scripture. They are wholly subordinate to the Bible.

Then why have creeds and confessions; what purpose do they serve?

There are large segments of professing Christianity that consider themselves anti-creedal and anti-confessional. They assert that such documents detract from the sole sufficiency of Scripture. Their great motto is, "No creed but the Bible."

As already noted, creedal and confessional churches do not deny the sole sufficiency of Scripture but diligently cherish this truth. Also, the statement, "No creed but the Bible," is in itself a creed. The overriding purpose of creeds and confessions is to clearly set forth what one believes about the Bible. Creeds and confessions are simply written down distinctives of belief in one given document. They provide a written summary for church members to read and know clearly what a church believes and why.

Where is "occurrent" found in the Bible?

"Occurrent" is a rare old English word that is found only once in the King James Version of the Bible. It is an adjective that signifies, "occurring," "current," "happening," "presenting itself" and, sometimes, "incidental." According to I Kings 5:4, King Solomon sent for Hiram, saying, "But now the LORD my God hath given me rest on every side, [so that there is] neither adversary nor evil occurrent."

Does the Bible say money is the root of all evil?

The Bible does not say, as is popularly supposed, that money is the root of all evil. It says that the *love* of money is the root of all evil, which is a different thing. I Timothy 6:10 says, "For the love of money is a root of all sorts of evil, and some by longing for it have wondered away from the faith, and pierced themselves with many a pang."

Is the last book in the Bible Revelations?

The correct title of the last book in the Protestant Bible is *The Revelation of St. John the Divine*. In popular usage it is called the *Book of Revelation* or the *Apocalypse*. Roman Catholics prefer to call it the *Apocalypse*, while Protestants generally call it the *Book of Revelation*. Often it is erroneously called the Book of Revelations or simply Revelations. In this connection *Revelation* should be singular, not plural, but the plural Revelations has been used so long and so widely in ordinary speech that it would be little short of pedantry to take exception to it now. *Apocalypse* comes to us through Latin from a Greek verb meaning, "to uncover," "disclose" or "reveal" and is virtually synonymous with "revelation."

Was the patriarch Job a Hebrew?

There is nothing in The Book of Job or elsewhere in the Bible to indicate that Job was a Hebrew. Like Melchizedek, Jethro and Balaam, Job occurs in the Bible as one of those scattered few who worshipped the true God but who were not connected with Israel. The usual assumption is that Job was and Arab chieftain.

What does the number 666 signify?

Six hundred sixty-six, often called the apocalyptic number, is the number given to one of the allegorical beasts seen by St. John the Divine in his vision on the island of Patmos. Revelation 13:18 says, "Here is wisdom. Let him who has understanding calculate the number of the beast, for the number is that of a man: and his number is six hundred and sixty-six."

This verse probably has given rise to more speculation than any other single passage in the Bible. The interpretations are many and varied. The symbolic and mystic number of the beast is often identified with the antichrist. It appears that at the time Revelation was written there was a tradition that an adversary of Christ, known as the antichrist, would appear. For instance, I John 1:18 says, "Children it is the last hour; and just as you heard that antichrist is coming, even now many antichrists have arisen; from this we know that it is the last hour."

There are allusions, though not direct references to the antichrist in Paul's Epistles. Probably the author of Revelation intended the number 666 (although some ancient manuscripts read 616) as an allusion to a particular person who would be recognizable to an inner circle of readers, but not to outsiders.

The cryptic number is most often identified with the Roman Emperor Nero. For generations after the death of Nero there was persistent belief that he was not actually dead and that he would return to govern the Roman Empire. In Greek, Nero was known as *Neron Kaiser* (Nero Caesar). In the almost vowel-less Hebrew of that day this name became, *Nron Ksr*. These letters correspond to the numerals 50, 200, 6, 50, 100, 60, and 200, which, when added together, total 666, the number of the beast. This ingenious device was accepted by many as conclusive proof that the beast was Nero.

Some, however, despite the statement in Revelation that the number "is that of a man," took the mystic number to refer to Rome itself rather than any particular person. Others throughout the centuries have used odd and far-fetched cryptic numerology to erroneously identify various persons of international significance with the number of the beast.

Is a law to themselves in the Bible?

This proverbial phrase is in the Bible. But it is used in a favorable rather than an unfavorable way, and it argues for the existence of "natural law." In Romans 2:14 & 15, Paul says "For when the Gentiles who do not have the Law do instinctively the things of the Law, these, not having the Law, are *a law to themselves*, in that they show the work of the Law written in their hearts, their conscience bearing witness, and their thoughts alternately accusing or else defending them."

How many times does the word *and* occur in the King James Version of the Bible?

The conjunction *and* occurs in the King James Version of the Bible 46,227 times, 35,543 times in the Old Testament and 10,684 times in the New Testament. The monotonous repetition of *and* in that and other English translations of the Bible is owing to the fact that the translators attempted to render the Hebrew and Greek originals as literally as possible.

Does the Bible mention holy water?

Holy water occurs only once in the various Protestant translations of Bible. It is found in Numbers 5:17 in connection with "the law of jealousies." Presumably this holy water was water from the tabernacle laver in which the priests performed their ritual washing before approaching the alter. In the Christian church holy water as a sacramental blessed by a priest to invoke God's blessing on those whose use it is believed to date from about the second century.

Is Esther, the biblical book underlying Purim, a comedy?

Many liberal religious scholars have reached the conclusion that the book of Esther is, fiction, - burlesque or farce, low comedy, that employed exaggeration, coincidences, improbabilities and verbal humor. In my opinion these scholars clearly miss the point that redemptive history takes place within the context of ordinary time. With God there is no linear dimension to time and redemptive history has a transcendent and vertical dimension to it. In redemptive history the eternal intersects the temporal, the infinite God touches our finite horizontal dimension of time.

The Old Testament gives us multiple examples of the intersection of redemptive history with secular history. One such example is seen in the narrative history of Esther, who was born at the precise second and in the precise place that God had ordained from the foundation of the world.

It is true that there were several problems with the Jewish canonization of the book. Except in Roman Catholic versions of the Bible, the name of God is nowhere found in the book of Esther's 167 verses (yet the King of Persia is mentioned 190 times), Esther was married to a non-Jew, and Purim was a pagan festival. Yet it is a most popular book among Jews. It is the only book (beside the Pentateuch) that has two Aramaic translations; there are more medieval manuscripts of Esther than any other Old Testament book; and its record of deliverance encourages readers to expect a similar deliverance.

Yet even without the name of God mentioned, the book of Esther displays a profound faith in Providence. The Hand of God, which is hardly burlesque or low comedy, is seen throughout its reading.

In the story of Esther, the king of Persia made a seven-day feast and summoned his queen, Vashti, to present herself to the dignitaries assembled to display her beauty. Vashti refused and she was forever forbidden to come before the king again. What followed was an attempt to find a suitable replacement for the queen. A spectacular beauty pageant was held and a young Jewish girl named Esther becomes Queen. (Liberal scholarship's primary argument for the book of Esther being fiction rests on the point that secular history contains no record of a Jewish queen in Persia. Since Esther could not reveal her nationality, why would there be a record, outside of the Bible, of a Jewish Queen in Persia?) Esther then "happens" to be in a position to counter a villainous plot to exterminate her people. Yes God is nowhere mentioned in the story, but God is everywhere implied in a series of "non-coincidences" throughout the book. Esther "happens" to win the beauty contest to become queen; her uncle Mordecai "happens" to foil a plot to kill the king; wicked Haman "happens" to be hung on the gallows he prepared for Mordecai.

Some argue that the book of Esther contains no ritual or other Jewish religious practices. I guess they must have skipped those passages that speak of the Jewish people responding to the lethal decree of the king by fasting. This fasting implies the belief in and reliance upon God. If the Jewish people had no hope of surviving, why would they fast? They would eat drink and be merry for tomorrow they die. This was no time for Esther and her maidens to go on a crash diet! The fast was a way of the Jewish people reaching out (as they often did throughout the Old Testament) to God, of humbling themselves and acknowledging complete dependence upon Him. God's Providence is everywhere demonstrated throughout the book of Esther, and that the people's only hope was in God is also implied in the passages on fasting.

Today Purim is celebrated as a noisy and fun festival. True, some view it as a kind of Jewish April Fool's Day. Perhaps the humor is in keeping with the irony of how God "chose" to preserve His people during the time, and particularly how He elevated the humble Mordecai and Esther and brought down the proud Haman. It is a story that calls us to remember the serious danger the Jewish people faced, and remembers the necessity of total dependence upon God's preserving power.

Why does a good God allow all this evil and suffering?

The Bible is filled with the cries of people, including the biblical authors, who are deeply perplexed and baffled by the magnitude and the unjust distribution of instances of evil and suffering. The problem may not be regarding belief in whether there is a God or not, but it may tempt you to mistrust, resent, or even hate God. Many thinkers have said that evil and suffering pose a powerful argument against belief in the very existence of the all-powerful good God.

The classic theoretical objection goes like this: "Is God willing to prevent evil but not able? Then God is impotent. Is God able to prevent evil, but not willing? Then God is malevolent, and not good. If God is both able and willing, then how can there be evil?" Dr. Timothy Keller of Redeemer Presbyterian Church in NYC points out that this objection hinges on a fallacious premise. It assumes that a good God would not have any good reason allow evil to continue. Just because we as mere mortals cannot think that God cannot have a good reason that does not mean that God could not have one. We say it is reasonable to assume that God is great enough to stop evil, but not great enough to have a good reason for allowing evil. We can't have it both ways.

Not only does this argument against God from evil not succeed, it actually has a boomerang effect. If there is a God then evil creates a grave personal problem. Why does God allow suffering to exist? But if there is no God, then you do not really have a good basis for being outraged at the existence of suffering. You can only object to injustice if you already believe in some kind of ethical standard, some supernatural standard that comes from outside of nature and judges some types of natural behavior as good or bad. And where does such a supernatural standard come from if not from God? There is no cogent argument that evil and suffering are incompatible with the existence of a holy and all powerful God.

An atheist has no rational basis to even be outraged at suffering and evil. What confirmation do Christians have that God has some good reason for allowing suffering and evil to "temporarily" continue? ***The Cross-!*** God must hate evil too, or He would not have done that and He must have some good reason for letting history continue too. Confidence in the character of God, His love, His justice, His wisdom, becomes possible only when we see what He did in coming to die on the cross to halt the greatest evil and suffering of all, separation from Him.

What does "Corban" mean?

We find the term Corban in Mark 7:10 and 11 which reads, "For Moses said, 'Honor your father and your mother' and, 'He who speaks evil of father or mother. Let him be put to death;' but you say, 'If a man says to his father or his mother, anything of mine you might have been helped by is Corban (that is to say, given to God).'" Corban is an Anglicized form of the Hebrew "qorban," literally meaning, "that which is brought near."

In the Hebrew Bible the term signifies "a special offering," "gift," or "oblation" and is so translated in the English Bible except in the passage just quoted. Later "Corban" was applied to any gift set apart for God, especially in performance of a vow, and therefore not to be appropriated to any other use.

In New Testament times "Corban" was little more than a formula for making a vow. For instance when a devout Jew said, "Corban to me is wine for a year, " he meant that he vowed to abstain from wine for that period. Or a son might say to his parents, "Corbon is whatever you might have profited by me," signifying that he vowed not to help them no matter what their need. Technically, whatever the son might have given his parents was dedicated as a gift to God. By this legal fiction the son could avoid his family responsibilities while doing a formal religious act. The scribes held that such a vow excused the son from giving to his parents what he had dedicated to God. Jesus clearly implies that some who had no intention of delivering the Corban to God adopted this device merely to avoid complying with the commandment and shirking their parental responsibilities.

Does the term Holy Ghost occur in the Old Testament?

In the King James Version of the Bible, the term Holy Ghost occurs more than eighty times in the New Testament, but not once in the Old Testament. The term Holy Spirit is used several times in the Old Testament for certain phases of action of God upon nature and man. "Cast me not away from thy presence; and take not thy holy spirit from me," says Psalms 51:11. Isaiah 63:10-11 says, "But they rebelled, and vexed his holy Spirit: therefore he was turned to be their enemy, and he fought against them. Then he remembered the days of old, Moses, and his people, saying, 'Where is he that brought them up out of the sea with the shepherd of his flock? Where is he that put his Holy Spirit within him?'"

Both the terms Holy Spirit and Holy Ghost occur in the New Testament. For instance, in Luke 11:13 Jesus is quoted as saying, "If ye then, being evil, know how to give good gifts unto your children: how much more shall your heavenly Father give the Holy Spirit to them that ask him?"

Who divided the Bible into chapters and verses?

Early editions in the Bible were not divided into chapters or into the small sections now known as verses. They did not contain even perceptible spaces between words. The division into chapters and verses was a gradual process that started during the Middle Ages.

Tertullian, who died before 240 A. D., referred to some sort of sections in the New Testament. Later the Gospels would be divided into what were known as the Ammonian-Eusebian sections, which were smaller divisions than our present chapters. Euthalius, a deacon and bishop who lived around the middle of the 5th century, divided parts of the New Testament into minute portions similar to the present verses. Around 1226 Cardinal Hugo de Sancto-Caro of France divided the entire Latin Vulgate into chapters and verses somewhat similar to those of today.

But even the early printed Bibles, such as the Guttneberg Bible, were not divided into chapters and verses. The first printed New Testament with such divisions was issued in 1527 at Lyons by Sanctus Pagninus. Robert Stephens followed a similar arrangement in his edition of the New Testament printed at Geneva in 1551. This was a two-volume work with the Greek text in the center of the page and with the Latin of Erasmus on one side and the Latin Vulgate on the other. Stephens, whose French name was Robert Estienne, was a member of a great family of scholars and printers in France. In the preface to his concordance, the son of Robert Stephens says his father worked out the system of chapters and verses for his edition of the New Testament while he was journeying on horseback from Paris to London.

This system of dividing the Bible into chapters and verses was adopted by William Whittingham (the husband of John Calvin's sister or sister-in-law) and his associates in the Geneva Bible (sometimes called the Breeches Bible). The Geneva Bible New Testament was first printed in 1557 and its Old Testament in 1560. An introductory note to the reader of that Bible says: "The argumentes bothe for the booke and for the chapters with the numbre of the verses are added."

The Geneva Bible is the first English version with the chapter and verse enumeration, as we know them. It should be borne in mind that the Greek classics and other ancient books were likewise arbitrarily divided into sections for convenience and reference. The general plan appears to have been to include each separate sentence or its equivalent in a verse, but this plan was not always followed.

Both chapters and verses often disregard natural divisions of thought and are misleading. For instance, the first three verses of Genesis 2 are clearly the conclusion of the narrative in Genesis 1. But the chapters and verses are now definitely fixed and are regarded as virtual parts of the Bible. Although the arrangement sometimes obscures the sense and interrupts the flow of the narrative, it is so convenient for reference and citation that its elimination would destroy the usefulness of thousands of concordances and other reference books and make millions of citations meaningless. The Revisers of 1885 tried to solve this problem by printing the chapter and verse numbers in the margin. This revision had little appeal.

Who was the first convert to Christianity in Europe?

So far as the Bible informs us, a woman named Lydia at Philippi in Macedonia was the first convert made to Christianity in Europe. Acts 16:14-15 says: "And a certain woman named Lydia, from the city of Thyatira, a seller of purple fabrics, a worshiper of God, was listening; and the Lord opened her heart to respond to the things spoken by Paul. And when she and her household had been baptized, she urged us, saying, 'If you have judged me to be faithful to the Lord, come into my house and stay.' And she prevailed upon us." After Paul and Silas were scourged, imprisoned and set free by divine power, they entered the house of Lydia.

Paul does not once refer to Lydia by name in all his epistles, a fact that suggests it may not have been her personal name, but the designation of her native country, since she came from Thyatira in *Lydia* in Asia Minor. It is generally assumed, however, that there were many Christian converts among the Jews in Rome and perhaps elsewhere in Europe before Paul visited that continent.

Why are the Ten Commandments called the Decalogue?

The Hebrew words in the Bible rendered Ten Commandments in English literally signify ten words. In the Septuagint, the Greek version of the Old Testament made at Alexandria in the second century B.C., this phrase was translated dekolagoi, from deka, "ten," and logos, "word." From this circumstance, the Ten Commandments collectively as a body of law and as the basis of the ethical system and religion of both Judaism and Christianity came to be known in the Western world as the Decalogue.

What are the Ten Commandments (or Decalogue) and where are they found?

Few people are able to quote the Ten Commandments for the simple reason that no set of commandments is specifically listed and numbered as the "ten commandments" in the Bible. Consequently there is no general agreement as to what exactly constitutes the "ten commandments."

The phrase, "ten commandments," however, occurs several times in the Old Testament. Exodus 34:28 says in part that Moses wrote upon the tables the words of the covenant, the ten commandments," and Deuteronomy 4:13 and 10:4 also mentions the "ten commandments."

It is generally assumed that Moses wrote down the law as a whole revealed by God to Moses on Sinai shortly after the Exodus from Egypt, while the Ten Commandments were inscribed by God Himself on the two tablets of stone. But the Ten Commandments are nowhere listed in the Bible as ten distinct and separate commandments. They are not found in the Scriptures arranged in the simple and orderly form in which they are usually circulated for popular use. By general agreement, these Ten Commandments that God wrote on the two tablets of stone are contained in Exodus 20:2-17 and Deuteronomy 5:6-18. From these two passages, which are practically identical, it may be seen how difficult it is to divide the words and thoughts into ten separate commandments. It is small wonder that different authorities have differed on the subject through the ages.

Naturally the form of the Ten Commandments given in Exodus is assumed to be older that that given in Deuteronomy, because the latter is in the nature of a recapitulation. Even Jewish authorities themselves have differed as to exactly which commandment should be regarded as the tenth. Jewish authorities, following Philo and Josephus generally regard Exodus 20:2 as the first of the Ten Commandments and many Protestant churches also follow that format. On the other hand, the Roman Catholic Church and Martin Luther (and consequently Lutheran churches) regard the first commandment as extending from verses 2 to 6. Likewise Jewish authorities and many Protestant churches regard the whole of Exodus 20:17 as constituting the tenth commandment, while the Roman Catholic and Lutheran churches regards that verse as comprising both the ninth and tenth commandments, thus technically distinguishing the coveting of a neighbor's wife from coveting his property.

In the Septuagint, the Greek version of the Old Testament made at Alexandria in the second century B.C., the phrase "ten commandments" was translated *dekalogoi* from *deka*, "ten" and *logos*, "word." The Ten Commandments, related in 120 Hebrew words have exercised a profound influence upon the religion, moral and social life of man. From this circumstance the Ten Commandments came to be known in the Western world as the Decalogue.

Is Hallelujah in the Bible?

Hallelujah in that form is not in the King James Version of the Bible. In it's Greek form Alleluia it occurs in Revelation 19:6, which reads; "And I heard as it were the voice of a great multitude, and as the voice of many waters, and as the voice of mighty thunderings, saying, Alleluia: for the Lord omnipotent reigneth." The Hebrew original of Hallelujah literally means, "Praise ye Yah," where Yah is the shortened form of the divine name, YHWH or "Yahweh."

In the Hebrew texts of the Old Testament in occurs at the opening of eleven Psalms and at the close of thirteen Psalms, but in each case the King James Version renders it "Praise ye the Lord," which is an approximation to the literal meaning.

From its frequent occurrence in the Hebrew original of the Psalms, Hallelujah has been widely adopted in Christian hymns and liturgies. It is supposed that was not originally an integral part of the Psalms in which it now occurs, but rather a liturgical or traditional ejaculation used with them.

Does the ancient existence of dinosaurs contradict the Bible?

Some Bible critics will use the fossil records of dinosaurs as proof that the Bible has errors. After all, they reason, since the Bible does not speak of dinosaurs and yet their existence has been proven, the Bible cannot be trusted as a historical account. However, a closer look at the Bible will show that the Bible may indeed speak of dinosaurs as creatures that were in existence at the time of the writing of some of the earliest writings of Scripture.

None of the common scientific names for dinosaurs are found in the Bible because the Bible predates the naming of phyla and classes by thousands of years. Yet there are references to beasts within Scripture that meet the physical requirements to be considered giant reptiles.

In Job 41, the Lord Himself describes a beast (Leviathan) that He formed that was physically huge and resembles something very reptilian. The Leviathan is mentioned again (in a figurative sense) in Isaiah 27:1, "In that day the Lord will punish Leviathan the fleeing serpent, with His fierce and great and mighty sword, even Leviathan the twisted serpent; and He will kill the dragon who lives in the sea."

There are several other references in Scripture of some great creatures of which we may never see the likes (e.g. Psalm 104:26). But all this begs the question of what happened to them?

There are some viable explanations regarding the disappearance of dinosaurs that square with the Genesis account of Noah's Flood. One theory is that all the dinosaurs were lost in the Flood, which would also account for the preservation of near-perfect skeletal/fossil remains. One problem with this argument is that Noah was commanded to take a pair of every unclean animal aboard the Ark, which would include all reptilian life. So at least two of every species of dinosaur (if they existed at that time) would have been taken on the Ark and thus have been present on the post-flood Earth.

What really happened to these magnificent creatures? Some have concluded that when the Earth underwent many changes to its climate after the Flood, the dinosaurs were unable to adapt to the temperature extremes and died. There are many other theories as well. Another says that a global viral infection wiped out the entire population of dinosaurs. In any event, not having all the answers says nothing about the evidence of the Bible and fossil records.

What is the longest word in the Bible?

The longest word in the King James Version of the Bible is Mahershalalhashbaz, which contains 18 letters. It occurs in Isaiah 8:1-4 where it appears as a word and a name. Mahershalalhashbaz is really a Hebrew sentence literally meaning, "the booty hastens, the spoil speeds." The prophet so named one of his sons either actually or figuratively to indicate the impending doom of Syria and Samaria.

Why aren't quotation marks used in the King James Version of the Bible?

Quotation marks originated in France during the latter part of the 16th century but had not generally been adopted by English printers when the King James Version of the Bible was first issued in 1611. Although quotation marks have been introduced in later English versions, they have never been inserted in the King James Version. Before the introduction of quotation marks there were no uniform signs in writing and printing to mark the beginning and end of matter borrowed from other books or sources. Quotations in the Bible are often introduced by such phrases as, "it is written," "it is said," "the scripture saith," "it was said to them of old time," etc. The number of explicit quotations from the Old Testament in the New Testament is estimated at 275. In the King James Version it is often difficult to tell exactly where a quotation begins and where it ends.

What chapter in the Bible ends with a comma?

Acts 21 is the only chapter in the King James Version and most other recognized English versions of the Bible that ends with a comma. In the standard French translations this chapter closes with a colon. Most all other chapters in English versions of the Bible end with periods, although there are several that end with question marks or exclamation points. The Book of Jonah, for instance, ends with a question mark.

Is "a law unto themselves" in the Bible?

This proverbial phrase is in the Bible, but it is used in a favorable rather than an unfavorable sense. In Romans 2:14 Paul says, "For when the Gentiles, which have not the law, do by nature the things contained in the law, these, having not the law, are a law unto themselves."

Does the Bible mentioned handling snakes?

In 1942, three members of a backwoods church in Kentucky were held to grand jury on a murder charge for participating in a meeting at which another member of the congregation was fatally bitten by rattlesnakes. The judge ordered the sheriff's deputies to kill four large rattlesnakes that were alleged to have bitten the murdered man while being handled at a religious meeting in the church.

Incidents of this kind have occurred in certain sections of Virginia, North Carolina, Tennessee and Kentucky. They became so frequent in Kentucky that the Kentucky legislature in 1940 passed a law making it illegal to use snakes in religious ceremonies.

The religious groups who make a practice of handling snakes in church are sometimes referred to as a snake cult. This creates the impression that these people are snake worshipers and that they indulge in snake charming. But snake charming and snake worship are not involved in this particular practice. These people interpret certain passages in the New Testament very literally, and undertake to put them into practice.

In Mark 16 it is related that Jesus after the Crucifixion, appeared to the eleven Apostles as they sat at meat and unbraided them for their unbelief and hardness of heart, because they did not believe those who had seen Him after He had risen from the grave. Jesus told the eleven that certain signs would follow them that believe, and one of the signs would be that they could take up serpents, and if they drank any deadly thing, it would not hurt them. According to Luke 10:19, Jesus told the seventy, after they returned, that they were given authority to tread upon serpents and scorpions, and to have power over the enemy, and nothing would injure them.

The viper story in Acts 28 tells of Paul being taken in bonds from Jerusalem to Rome. The ship of Alexandria sailing to Italy from Myra, a city of Lycia was run aground during a storm on the shores of Melita (modern Malta). In verses 2 through 6 we read of Paul placing a bundle of sticks on the fire and a viper coming out of the heat and fastening on his hand. But when the natives saw the creature hanging from his hand, they began saying to one another, "undoubtedly this man is a murderer, and though he has been saved from the sea, justice has not allowed him to live." However Paul shook the creature off into the fire and suffered no harm. After a long time, when the natives noticed that nothing unusual happened to Paul, they changed their minds and began to say that he was a god.

Some authorities have questioned his story on the ground that there are no venomous reptiles of any kind on the island of Malta at the present time. Be that as it may, the snake handlers of the mountains and Kentucky and neighboring states accept these passages in the Bible literally and a sincerely believe that if their Christian faith is firm enough they can tread on and take up with their bare feet and hands rattlesnakes, copperheads another poisonous snakes without being harmed. They do not worship snakes, or charm them, or exercise any power over them, but simply use them to put their own faith to the utmost test.

The orthodox and my position maintain that while the Bible is literally true, it is so only within the context in which it was written and picking up snakes is something no responsible interpreter would say should be true of every Christian. It is also very probable that that verse in Mark was not part of Mark's original gospel since many early and very reliable manuscripts do not include Mark 16:9-20. Therefore, its doubtful status means that it is a precarious basis upon which to build a doctrine of snake handling.

Does God exist?

My answer may surprise you, but from a strict theological and philosophical perspective, God does not exist. Unless we stop to realize how sovereign, majestic and awesome God is, we frequently unwittingly delimit Him. One such example is when we say God exists. God does not exist.

You and I exist, but God does not exist. We exist because there was a time when we did not exist. To say that God exists, would mean that there was a time when God did not exist. If God merely exists, the question raised would be how did He come to exist. He could not have created Himself. To create Himself, He would have had to exist before He existed. God would have to be, before He is. God would have to exist and not exist at the same time.

The very concept of self-creation is totally irrational. As children we often would ask, "Who made God?" and then someone would answer, "God made Himself." God could not have made Himself. Saying that God self-exists does not involve any contradiction and is not irrational.

It is true that every effect must have a cause, but every cause does not have to have a cause. God's self-existence simply means that there was no time when God started to exist. This attribute of God means that He self-exists for which theologians use the term aseity (from the Latin words a se, which mean "from himself"). Other beings come to be, but only God self-exists.

To exist is to participate in being. We do not own "being" or possess it all by ourselves, but we have the privilege of participating in it. Our Creator who does own being grants that privilege to us. It is in Him that we live and move and have our being (Acts 17:28). Being belongs to God. It is part of His nature. He is being; He is pure being.

So you see God does not exist, God IS! He always has been. He is eternal. He has no beginning and no end. Nothing caused God to come into existence. He did not make Himself. He is not a creature; He is not dependent; He is not derived. He is independent, self-sufficient, and secure. God, and God alone has the power of being within Himself. He is who He is, the "I Am Who I Am." He alone is the source of all being, of all existence. Therefore, God does not exist. He Is!

Does God ever change his mind?

Theologians of the modern era have written much about a theology known as "Openness Theology," or about a God in process. Modern thinkers like Dr. Gregory A. Boyd, author of the excellent book, Letters From A Skeptic, is among those contemporary theologians now flirting with the idea of a finite God, a God who is a part of the process of change, growth, and development. Some years ago several issues of the publication Christianity Today also dealt with this subject.

In my opinion, and that of most theologians, the immutability of God is a necessary condition of His aseity or self-existence. Reason alone concludes that no change is possible in God, since a change is either for better or for worse. In God we have absolute perfection, therefore an improvement or deterioration are both equally impossible. This immutability of God is clearly stated in such Scripture verses as Ex. 3:14; Ps. 93; Ps. 102:26-28; Isa. 41:4, 48:12; Mal. 3:6; Rom. 1:23; Heb. 1:11, 12; and Jas. 1:17 to cite but a few passages.

At the same time there many passages of Scripture, which seem to ascribe change to God (Ex 32: 10-14; Jonah 3:10; Prov. 11:20, 12:22; and Psa. 18:26, 27 to cite a few). The apparent confusion here is based to a certain extent on misunderstanding. The divine immutability should not be understood as implying immobility, as if they were no movement in God. God is always in action. There is change roundabout Him, change in the relations of men to Him, but there is no change in His Being, His attributes, His purpose, His motives, or His promises. When Scripture speaks of His repenting, changing His intention, and altering His relation with sinners when they repent, we should remember that this is only an anthropomorphic way of speaking. The change is not in God, but in man and in man's relations to God. God's decisions are not dependent on the actions of man.

Einstein said God does not play dice with the universe. Neither are there maverick molecules running around the universe. A finite, changing, evolving God would be marred by an ever-turning shadow. He would be a chameleon. He would not necessarily be tomorrow what He is today, or today what He was yesterday.

The great theologian Dr. Emil Brunner stated in his book The Christian Doctrine of God (p. 269) that, "The idea of a 'God who becomes' is a mythological and unreal idea. Were God Himself One who is 'becoming' then everything would flounder in the morass of relativism. . . . The God of the Bible is eternally unchangeable."

What is meant by general and special revelation?

Believers know what they know about God deductively because of divine revelation. God has revealed Himself in two ways, by general revelation and by special revelation. Believers may deduce from these generalizations their particular knowledge of God.

General revelation means that God has given information about Himself in His entire creation through the power and focus of nature, the constitution of the human mind, in the voice of conscience, and in the facts of experience and of history (Psalms 19:1, 2; Romans 1:19, 20; 2:14, 15).

Special revelation is what is embedded in the Bible. The Holy Scriptures are central in the thinking and behavior of believers. The Bible is seen as the inspired and infallible Word of God (II Timothy 3:16). John Calvin commenting on this verse in his Commentaries on the Epistles of Timothy, Titus., and Philemon, says that "the Law and the Prophets are not a doctrine delivered according to the will and pleasures of men, but dictated by the Holy Spirit." What the writers of Scripture wrote was exactly what God wanted to convey (II Peter 1:20, 21). This means that the Bible is inspired in its historical archaeological and scientific facts as well as in its moral and religious teaching. The Bible is true, within the context in which it was written, in all that it affirms.

This inspiration extends not only to the entire Bible but also to the very words employed. Theologically this is referred to as plenary inspiration, which means that all the words of Scripture (in the original manuscripts) are God's

Words; every single word of Scripture is God-breathed. Jesus and Paul formulated arguments on the basis of a single word in Scripture (Matthew 22:43, 45; John 10:35; Galatians 3:16). Jesus applied the authority of Scripture to every jot and tittle of the Scriptures (Matthew 5:18).

Isn't the infallibility of the Bible a 17th. century myth? After all, the reformers never said the Bible was inerrant?

Both the Roman Catholic Church and the Reformers held that "sacred Scripture is the word of God" or "the voice of God." The authority of Scripture was never at issue during the Reformation. Therefore, there was never a need for the Reformers to give a lengthy discourse on inerrancy. The Fourth Session of the Council of Trent in the 16th. century confirmed that Scripture was a source of revelation. What was at issue was whether authority comes from Scripture alone or from Scripture and tradition.

While Luther and Calvin may never have used the word inerrant, Luther did say, "Scriptures are assigned to the Holy Ghost. In Scripture you are not reading the word of man but of the most exalted God. Scriptures have never erred." Calvin said, "Since no daily responses are given from heaven, and the Scriptures are the only records in which God has been pleased to consign His Truth in perpetual remembrance, the full authority which they ought to possess with the faithful is not recognized unless they are believed to have come from heaven directly as if God had been heard giving utterance to them." No 17th. century theologian ever gave a higher ascription to Scripture than these words that we have directly from the pens of Luther and Calvin.

Is it not arrogant to claim that Jesus is the only way to God?

It is important to understand that Christianity is not the only religion that claims exclusivity. Muslims radically claim exclusivity as well. They do so not just theologically but linguistically as well. Muslims believe that the sole, sufficient, and consummate miracle of Islam is the Koran and that it is only recognizable in Arabic. Any other translation "desacralizes" it.

Buddhism was born when Gautama Buddha rejected two fundamental assertions of Hinduism: the ultimate authority of Vedas (their scriptures) and the caste system. Hinduism is absolutely uncompromising on two or three issues. These are: the law of karma (which is the moral law of cause and effect so that every birth is a rebirth that makes recompense for the previous life), the authority of the Vedas, and reincarnation. Hinduism appears on the surface to be a tolerant faith in that it allows one to practice one's own religion as long as it buys into Hinduism's notion of truth, which is syncretistic. Syncretism is the attempt to blend together different or even opposing beliefs.

Sikhism challenged both Hinduism and Buddhism. Atheists reject the viewpoint of those who believe in God. Baha'ism claims to be the cosmic embrace of all religions and thus excludes the exclusivists. Therefore it is not true that Christianity is arrogant when it claims exclusivity; every other major religion does so as well.

All truth is by definition exclusive. If truth does not exclude, then no assertion of truth can be made. Truth excludes its opposite and anything contrary to it must be false.

What Biblical city was sown with salt?

Abimelech, one of the first Israelites to make himself a king, sowed the city of Shechem with salt after he had captured and destroyed the place following a revolt of the people. This story may be found in Judges 9:45.

Is Nazareth mentioned in the Old Testament?

The Old Testament does not mention Nazareth where Jesus spent most of His childhood, all of His youth and most of His manhood. It is believed that in the time of Jesus, chiefly Samaritans inhabited the village of Nazareth. From Luke 1: 26-27, and Luke 2:3-5, we may conclude that both Joseph and Mary lived there before their espousal. Matthew 2:22-23 indicates that after Joseph returned from Egypt to Israel with "the young child and His mother," Joseph and Mary had originally intended to settle in Bethlehem or elsewhere in Judea.

No prophecy saying that the Messiah should be called a Nazarene is found in the Old Testament. Some Jewish authorities suppose Nazarene here to be merely a play upon two Hebrew words translated *Branch*, a term applied by the old prophets to the Messiah. Jeremiah 23:5 speaks of the Lord raising unto David a righteous Branch, and in Isaiah 11:1 we read, "Then a shoot will spring from the stem of Jesse, and a Branch from his roots will bear fruit." At any rate, in consequence of the decision made by Joseph and Mary, their first-born child came to be known as "Jesus of Nazareth."

For some unknown reason Nazareth appears to have been held in contempt in the time of Jesus. In John 1:46 we find Nathanael asking if any good thing can come out of Nazareth?

Do Nazarene and Nazarite mean the same thing?

Nazarene and Nazarite are often confused. Nazarite occurs frequently in the Old Testament. It is from a Hebrew word meaning, "to dedicate" or "consecrate." Among the Israelites a Nazarite was a devotee or consecrated person who was prohibited from drinking wine, cutting the hair or touching a corpse. The conditions of being a Nazarite were subject to minute regulations. Although the term itself does not occur in the New Testament, some Biblical scholars suppose that both John the Baptist and St. Paul took the vows of a Nazarite. There is no evidence in the Bible that the vow taken by a Nazarite prohibited marriage. In fact we know that Samson, though a Nazarite, was married.

In Acts 24:5, where a certain orator named Tertullus, in his accusation against Paul before Felix at Jerusalem, is quoted as saying "For we have found this man a pestilent fellow, and a mover of sedition among all the Jews throughout the world, and a ringleader of the sect of the Nazarenes." It is merely a common rendering of the Greek word translated elsewhere as "of Nazareth." For some unknown reason Nazareth appears to have been held in contempt in the time of Jesus. We read in John 1:46, "And Nathanael said unto him, Can there any good thing come out of Nazareth? Philip saith unto him, Come and see." Also, it is barely possible that the reference to Jesus in Matthew 2:23, "And he came and dwelt in a city called Nazareth: that it might be fulfilled which was spoken by the prophets, He shall be called a Nazarene," is a mistake for, "He shall be called a Nazarite," since there is no Old Testament verse that exactly corresponds to this.

What was the slaughter of the innocents?

The slaughter of the innocents is the popular name given to the massacre of the infants by order of Herod the king in his attempt to destroy the young child Jesus, who was saved by being taken secretly into Egypt by Joseph and Mary. The phrase itself occurs nowhere in the Bible and the incident is related only in Matthew 2:16-18. That is the only information we have on the subject.

There is no reference whatever to this act of Herod in the history records of the time. Even Josephus, in his long, rather detailed and unfavorable accounts of the life of Herod the Great, does not mention it. It is particularly strange that Josephus would omit all reference to this cruel and brutal act when he takes such great pains to record so many barbarous enormities committed by Herod.

Although it is remarkable that the Roman authorities would have permitted the puppet king of Judea to commit such a wholesale slaughter of children, it is not doubted that Herod was capable of such cruelty and brutality. At the time he had, with the permission of Rome, put three of his own sons to death, was virtually insane, and was extremely suspicious of any person who might be mentioned as a possible successor to him as King of the Jews. Throughout centuries various commentators have estimated the number of children destroyed by Herod all the way from 150,000 to only a dozen. There is no information whatever on which to base such figures.

Since all the male children from two years old and under were destroyed, some authorities suppose this act of barbarity was committed about two years after the birth of Jesus. At an early date the Christian church recognized these innocent children slain by order of Herod as the first Christian martyrs, and Holy Innocents' Day, or Childermas (as it is called in England) is observed as a festival in the Roman Catholic Church on December 28 and in the Greek Orthodox Church on December 29 in commemoration of the massacre of the Holy Innocents.

Childermas, according to an old superstition, is the unluckiest day of the entire year. The coronation of Edward IV in 1461 was postponed a day to avoid having it fall upon this day of ill omen. In Great Britain the term "slaughter of innocents" is applied facetiously in Parliamentary circles to the bills left over at the end of a session for want of time.

What is the legend of Mohammed and the Mountain?

"If the mountain will not come to Mohammed, Mohammed must go to the mountain," has been a familiar English proverb since the seventeenth century. It is said of one who, unable to have things his own way, bows to the inevitable.

Apparently the proverb was suggested by a passage in Francis Bacon's essay "Of Boldness," in which he says: "You shall see a bold fellow many times do Mahomet's miracle. Mahomet made the people believe that he would call an (sic) hill to him, and from the top of it offer his prayers, for the observers of his law. The people assembled; Mahomet called the hill to come to him, again and again; and when the hill stood still, he was never a bit abashed, but said: If the hill will not go to Mahomet, Mahomet will go to the hill." No earlier reference to the story of Mohammed and the mountain has been produced, and no counterpart of it has been found in Moslem or Arabic literature.

The New Testament contains several references to mountain removing faith. "If you have faith as a grain of mustard seed, you shall say to this mountain, 'Move from here to there,' and it shall move" (Matthew 17:20). "If you have faith and do not doubt, you shall not only do what was done to the fig tree, but even if you say to this mountain, 'Be taken up and cast into the sea,' it shall happen" (Matthew 21:21, also Mark 11:23). "And if I have the gift of prophesy, and know all mysteries and all knowledge; and if I have all faith, so as to remove mountains, but do not have love, I am nothing" (I Corinthians 13:2). However, there is no occurrence of this figure of speech in the Koran or in pre-seventeenth century Moslem writings.

A story of later date than that of Bacon (and probably of English origin), says that when Mohammed first began to teach his doctrine to the Arabs, they demanded, as a sign of his divine authority, some miracle such as Moses, Jesus, and other prophets had performed. Mohammed at first replied that any such pretension to miraculous powers on his part would be displeasing to God. The Arabs persisted in their demand, whereupon Mohammed, to satisfy them, called to

Mt. Safa (a mountain near Mecca sacred to pagan Arabs) to come to him. When the mountain paid no attention to the prophet's command, he said: "God is merciful: for had the mountain obeyed my words and come to me, it would have fallen on us to our destruction: therefore I will go to the mountain and give thanks to God for showing mercy to a stiff-necked generation."

What is the doctrine of predestination and is it Biblical?

Predestination simply means that God, in His absolute sovereignty has pre-determined all eventual outcomes, hence our eternal destinies. When we turn to the Bible we find numerous emphatic statements about God's sovereign and gracious predestination, His election of believers. Here are just a few.

In Matthew 24:31 Jesus said His angels would gather His elect, His chosen ones from one end of heaven to the other. In John 15:16 Jesus said, "You did not chose Me, I chose you." In John 6:44 Jesus said, "No one can come to me unless the Father who sent me draws (literally drags) him."

Predestination also pervades the writings of Paul. In Ephesians 1:4 & 5, Paul wrote, "Just as He chose us in Him before the foundation of the world, that we should be holy and blameless before Him. In love He predestined us to adoption as sons through Jesus Christ to Himself, according to the kind intention of His will." In Ephesians 1:11 we read that we are "chosen from the beginning (or predestined) and all things happen just as He decided long ago." Throughout Paul's letters we find constant references to the elect, the predestined, the chosen or the called. In Romans 8: 29-30 Paul wrote, "For whom He foreknew, He also predestined . . . and whom He predestined, He also called." Luke in writing about the history of the early Church wrote in Acts 13:48 that "as many as had been ordained or appointed to eternal life believed."

The Old Testament also supports the doctrine of predestination. Psalm 65:4 says, "How greatly to be envied are those you have chosen." The entire 139 Psalm speaks of God's perfect knowledge of us. Verses 15 and 16 state, "You (that is God) were there when I was being formed in utter seclusion! You saw me before I was born and scheduled each day of my life before I began to breathe. Everyday was recorded in your Book!" Isaiah 55:11 states, "So shall My word be which goes forth from my mouth; It shall not return to me empty, Without accomplishing what I desire, And without succeeding *in the matter* for which I sent it."

Consider Peter's great confession of faith when he said to Jesus, "You are the Christ, the Son of the living God"? Jesus did not commend Peter for coming to that conclusion on his own intellect and his own merits. Instead Jesus said, "God has blessed you Simon, Son of Jonah, for my Father in heaven has personally revealed this to you – this is not from any human source." What Jesus was saying is that the recognition of who Jesus is came to Peter and comes to us, not from ourselves, but from God.

Do you agree with Martin Luther when he wrote, "free will is a nonentity" in The Bondage of The Will?

Yes I do. Free will is defined as the equal ability, under given circumstances, to choose either of two courses of action with no antecedent power determining the choice. Whatever motivations or inclinations one may have, or whatever inducements are laid before a person that might seem to turn the person in a certain direction, that person may at a moment disregard them all and do the opposite. Given this definition of free will, a will that produces our choices out of thin air, out of nothing, based on no controlling factors, is a will of the wisp; it is a nonentity. It makes no sense at all.

We do choose, but we always have a reason for the choices that we make. We have free choices in the sense that they are our personal choices, but they are not free in the sense that they are uninfluenced and undetermined by considerations. On the contrary, they are determined by influences and considerations that we find attractive or repulsive, as the case may be. We always act in accord with our strongest motivations and thus our wills are not free since they are controlled by these motivations. We act according to our disposition. We never make choice without reasons. We always choose according to what seems good to us. Thus, we are given the ability to make free choices, but our freedom is a limited freedom.

Even God in His absolute sovereignty, as He presents Himself to us in Scripture, limits Himself and does not have free will in the sense that it is defined in the first paragraph. God cannot act contrary to His own nature. God cannot sin. God cannot steal not only because everything He does is right, but also because He owns everything. There is no one to steal from. There is no law superior to God.

If we hold that God is sovereign and, as Scripture emphatically tells us, God foreknows and foreordains all things, then He can neither be deceived nor hindered in His all-knowing (prescience) and predestination, and that nothing can take place but according to His will, then, as Luther wrote, "there can be no free will in man, in angel or in any creature."

What is meant by the free will of man?

Though many secular determinists have denied the reality of will to human beings, that is not the case with historic Christianity. The issue in the church has been not so much whether we have wills, but the extent to which our wills are free. The issue in theology (as distinguished from philosophy, wherein the question of free will encounters other obstacles) has two aspects.

The first has to do with the relationship between man's will and God's will with respect to predestination and divine providence. Here, most agree (at least certainly Calvinists) that in the mystery of concurrence, or the point at which the human will intersects the divine will, man's freedom is neither violated nor destroyed. That is, the human will does not fall victim to coercion; God works out His divine will in and through the choices made by the human will. At no time does He reduce humans to the level of impersonal or non-volitional puppets who can move and act only as their strings are pulled externally. We are free but not autonomous.

The second aspect of theological concern regarding free will has to do with the degree to which our liberty has been impaired by "the Fall." This is the issue that was at the heart of the Pelagian controversy that pitted the British monk Pelagius against St. Augustine of Hippo in the fifth century. In that debate, Pelagius argued that man not only was created free but that his nature was created immutable. He denied the reality of the fall, arguing that Adam's sin affected Adam and only Adam. There was no fall into a state of moral corruption called original sin, which was transmitted to the entire human race.

Against Pelagius, Augustine argued that the fall produced dire consequences for humanity that involved the loss of original liberty. He distinguished between "free will" and "liberty." A better term for what he described as "free will" would be "free agency." Augustine argued that since the fall man still has a free will, or free agency — that is, he retains the faculty of choosing. He still can act intentionally, according to his desires. What he lost was any desire for the things of God. Thus, he never will choose God precisely because he doesn't want to choose God. This is freedom without liberty. This state of affairs is rooted in man's bondage to sin. The sinner is both free and enslaved at the same time, but not in the same relationship. We is free to do what we want, but what we want to do is sin. Therein is our bondage and the reason why Martin Luther wrote in his treatise, The Bondage of The Will, that "free will is a non-entity."

Pagan and humanistic views of man, even while admitting that we sin, do not agree that we sin because of a fallen nature that is enslaved to sin. Sin is seen as peripheral to human experience, not at its core. The humanist argues that a free will is always an indifferent will that has no pre-inclination to sin but is always able, in any circumstance, to choose sin or righteousness. It is this "indifference" that is on a collision course with the biblical view of man.

Who was the first woman to translate the Bible?

Julia Evelina Smith (1792-1886), of Glastonbury, Connecticut, translated the Bible into English from Latin, Greek and Hebrew and was the first woman to translate the entire Bible into any language. She started the project when she was 77 years old and completed it when she was 84. Her translation of the Bible was published in Hartford in 1876 at her own expense. She and her sister, Abby Hadassah Smith, were prominent abolitionists and advocates of women's rights. When Julia was 87 she married Amos A. Parker, who was 86. Their father, Zephaniah Smith, was originally a Congregational minister but quit the ministry because he decided preaching for pay was wrong.

What are the Synoptics?

Synoptics is the name that Bible scholars and critics apply to the three Gospels according to Matthew, Mark and Luke. The term, like synopsis, is derived from two Greek words meaning, "general view."

These first three Gospels are called Synoptic Gospels because they agree in many respects in subject matter, language, manner of treatment and point of view. Mark relates the public ministry of Jesus chiefly in Galilee and within a period of about a year, while Matthew and Luke, in the same general spirit, repeat much of Mark with many additional sayings of Jesus, incidents in His life, and other information. The fourth Gospel, the Gospel according to John, is written from an entirely different viewpoint and in a different style and spirit. John, unlike the Synoptics, places the scene chiefly in Jerusalem, emphasizes the Jewish festivals in connection with the public ministry of Jesus, and casts the subject matter in the form of symbolic discourses.

What is the Pentateuch?

Pentateuch is a word of Greek origin and literally means "the five books." It is derived from penta, "five," and teuchos, "tool, implement or vessel" and by extension "book." The term Pentateuch has been applied for many centuries by Bible critics and students to the first five books of the Old Testament, Genesis, Exodus, Leviticus, Numbers and Deuteronomy. Since this part of the Bible is traditionally ascribed to Moses, it is often referred to as "the five books of Moses."

The Jews call it "The Torah." Torah is a Hebrew word with a two-fold meaning. On the one hand it connotes "the law" and on the other it means "doctrine in the sense of teaching." In the later usage the first six books of the Old Testament are sometimes call the Hexateuch, signifying "the six books," because the sixth book, Joshua continues the same general account of the Israelites and is believed to be a part of the same literary production.

All five of the books of the Pentateuch received their current names from the Septuagint, the pre-New Testament Greek translation. For the most part the ancient Hebrew as well as the modern Jewish names for these books are quite different from the names they bear in our English copies. In many cases the Jewish names of the books of the Old Testament are merely the opening words. This same practice is followed by the Vatican in the naming of their certain bulls and edicts.

What are the meanings of the names of the books of the Pentateuch?

The meanings of the names of the books of the Pentateuch are as follows: Genesis, "creation"; Exodus, "the departure"; Leviticus, "the Levitical (book)," that is "the priestly book"; Numbers, "pertaining to the numbering of the Israelites"; Deuteronomy, "the second law." The original Greek names have been somewhat Latinized and even Angelicized in our English versions.

Where does the Bible say, "The Lord is a man of war?"

Exodus 15:3 says, "The Lord is a man or war (literally a warrior): the Lord is his name." This is part of the song that Moses and the children of Israel sang after the miraculous crossing of the Red Sea and the destruction of the Egyptian army.

Is Christianity a rational belief?

Christianity is indeed a rational belief, but true Christians are not rationalists. A rationalist is someone who embraces a philosophy that sets itself over and against Christianity. Christianity is coherent and intelligible. Christianity embraces a consistent pattern of truth; it does not indulge in superstition, and is based on a book, the Bible that is written for our understanding.

This does not mean that we can induce from a few general principles the complete majesty of all of its Truth. What we do know, we know because God has revealed such knowledge to us through His creation, through His prophets, through history, through the Bible and through His only begotten Son, Jesus Christ.

God does not ask us to abandon our minds. What He reveals to us is intelligible. This is not to say that everything in the Christian faith is absolutely clear with respect to rational categories. How a person can have a human nature and a divine nature at the same time, which is what we believe about Christ. Or how can we explain the mystery of the Trinity. These are mysteries in the same way that the ultimate force of gravity is a mystery, but they are not irrational.

Who cut Samson's hair?

It is a common mistake to suppose that Delilah with her own hands cut off the hair of Samson. Delilah did not do it herself but had someone else do it for her while Samson slept on her knees. The incident is recorded in Judges 16:19.

Who killed Sisera?

It is another common mistake to suppose that Deborah killed Sisera, the commander of the army of Jabin the King of Canaan, but it was actually Jael who killed him. The story may be found in fourth chapter of Judges.

Does the word "science" occur in the Bible?

The word "science" occurs twice in the King James Version of the Bible, once in each testament. In the Old Testament we find the word in Daniel 1:4. The Hebrew word here translated "science" signifies insight or understanding.

In the New Testament we find the word in I Timothy 6:20. Here "science" is the English translation of the Greek word *gnosis*, meaning knowledge. Here it refers to pseudo-science, false knowledge, the speculative systems of those claiming to possess superior esoteric learning.

Does the Bible forbid women to wear men's clothes?

The interchange of attire between men and women is forbidden in the Mosaic law, in Deuteronomy 22:5. This provision may have alluded to certain heathen rites practiced in Syria in which men and women among the idolatrous worshippers exchanged dress. St. Paul, however, who was raised a strict Jew and was familiar with the Mosaic law, may have been influenced by this passage in arriving at the conclusion that it was improper for women to imitate men in worshipping with their heads uncovered as he expounds in First Corinthians 11:3-16.

What does neesing mean?

Neesing is an obsolete word that occurs in the King James Version once. According to Job 41:18, the Lord, answering the patriarch, said of the leviathan (crocodile), "By his neesings a light doth shine, and his eyes are like the eyelids of the morning." Neesing is related to sneezing in other versions of the Bible. We find the word sneezed appearing only once in the King James Version. According to II Kings 4:35, when Elisha restored the son of the Shunamite woman to life "the child sneezed seven times."

Does the Bible mention cabins?

Cabins occurs only once in the King James Version. In Jeremiah 27:16 we are told that the prophet entered "into the dungeon, and into the cabins." There cells express the correct meaning, and it is so translated in other versions.

Where does the Bible mention frying pan?

Frying pan occurs twice in the King James Version. Leviticus 2:7 says, "And if thy oblation be a meat offering baken in the frying pan, it shall be made of fine flour with oil." Again, Leviticus 7:9, "And all the meat offering that is baken in the oven, and all that is dressed in the frying pan, and in the pan, shall be the priest's that offereth it." Just what the frying pan was is not known. The Hebrew original, so translated, probably means simply a shallow vessel either of earthenware or metal.

Why does the anchor symbolize hope?

The anchor as the symbol of hope was suggested by Hebrew 6:19, which reads in part, "This hope we have as an anchor of the soul." Hope is the motto of Rhode Island and the chief figure in the design on the flag of that state is an anchor. Anchors are only mentioned two other times in the Bible, both in Acts 27:29 and 30. In connection with Paul's voyage from Caesarea to Malta we read, "And fearing that we may run aground somewhere on the rocks, they cast four anchors from the stern and wished for daybreak. And as the sailors were trying to escape from the ship, and had let down the ship's boat into the sea, on the pretense of intending to lay out anchors from the bow." Originally large stones were used to hold ships at anchor, but in Paul's time the Romans already used anchors of metal similar to those in use at the present time.

Does the Bible say Luke was a physician?

Our information that Luke, reputed author of the third Gospel and of the Book of Acts, was a doctor by profession rests solely upon a single phrase used by Paul. In Colossians 4:14 the Apostle to the Gentiles calls Luke, "the beloved physician." It is supposed that Luke was a native of Antioch and was a Gentile Christian of Greek culture.

There is nothing improbable in the statement that Luke was a physician. Some authorities think this is borne out by internal evidence in the writings ascribed to him, such as his use of medical terms and his emphasis upon mercy and the healing art. Others, however, say that Luke's references to these matters are no more than could be expected of any person of Greek culture who was possessed of the general scientific, philosophical, theological and artistic knowledge of the time.

Paul is believed to have suffered throughout life from some physical affliction. If that is true, what would be more natural than for him to take as the companion on his missionary journeys a Greek doctor who had early become an adherent of the new faith? Nor is there anything improbable in the church legend that Luke was also a painter and sculptor. A picture of the Virgin found in Jerusalem and now in Rome is traditionally attributed to him. There is no evidence that Luke ever knew Jesus personally.

What is the significance of the Dead Sea Scrolls?

In 1947 huge clay pots were discovered in the caves of QUMRAN on the shore of the Dead Sea. These pots contained pieces of scrolls with ancient Hebrew writing, written between 200 BC and 100 AD. They contained the text of many Old Testament books, which confirmed the accuracy of our later translations of the Bible. Most significant is that it provided additional evidence for the conservative view that God's Word, through the Scriptures, has been handed down faithfully. In addition, these scrolls gave us more knowledge about the world in which Jesus lived.

Some biblical scholars have referred to Jesus' reluctance in the Synoptic Gospels (Matthew, Mark and Luke) to let His identity as the Son of God be known, as the "Messianic Secret." What is meant by that phrase?

Scholars have suggested that Jesus wanted the demons to be silent because: (1) The people were not ready to receive the news of who He was, or (2) He did not want the word coming from them, or (3) He was afraid the people would understand His mission in terms of the popular concept of the Messiah instead of the spiritual concept which He was going to fulfill. Scholars refer to this reluctance on Jesus' part to let His identity to be known as the "Messianic Secret."

The term began when W. Wrede, in his book, The Messianic Secret, (published in 1963) attempted to explain why Jesus never proclaimed Himself as the Messiah. Wrede wrote that Jesus did not reveal Himself as such until the resurrection. This would historically refute Peter's great confession in Mark's Gospel. Other scholars suggest Mark's "Messianic Secret" existed to avoid offending Rome.

Are Christians being egotistical and intolerant when they say Jesus is the only way to God?

The only way a statement can be egotistical and intolerant is if someone holds something to be true only because it is what he or she believes. That is, it is egotistical only when one maintains something is true merely because one decides to believe that it is true.

Christians believe that Jesus Christ is God incarnate because Jesus said that He is God divine. Jesus said, "I am the way, the truth and the life. No one comes to the Father except through me" (John 14:6). Therefore, are we to conclude that Jesus Christ is an egotistical bigot?

If by restating what Jesus Christ Himself said makes Christians egotistical bigots, then Jesus Christ is Himself an egotistical bigot. It seems odd that Christians who stand up for what Jesus Christ said about Himself are accused of being intolerant bigots, while those who make such accusations are not accused of being intolerant of Christian beliefs.

How did the Dead Sea get its name?

The name Dead Sea does not occur in the Bible. The Apostolic Fathers and other early post-biblical writers were the ones who first applied that name to the lowest body of water in the world. Its normal level is about 1300 feet below the Mediterranean. Given its depth of 1300 feet, this means that its bottom is nearly 2600 feet below sea level making it the deepest natural depression on the face of the earth.

In the Bible it is called "the salt sea," "the eastern sea" and "the sea of the plain." A tradition dating back about 1900 years says the Dead Sea covers the site of the wicked cities destroyed by Jehovah with brimstone from heaven.

Josephus refers to the Dead Sea as "the lake called Asphaltitis," from which we get our word asphalt. The Arabs call this body of water Bahr Lut, "lake of Lot," in allusion to the fact that Lot's wife was turned into a pillar of salt on its desolate shores.

The Dead Sea deserves its name. Its waters are so salty that no fish, animal or plant life (except a few algae) is able to live in them. The water is about four times as salty as seawater and is so buoyant that a human body will not sink in it.

The sea receives the Jordan and other waters but unlike other bodies of water, has no outlet. Because the Dead Sea only receives from other waters and does not give, it is the most desolate and dreary region in the world. There is an obvious parable being shown to us by this body of water.

How is YHVH or YHWH pronounced?

The name for the Heavenly Father in the original Hebrew Scriptures is represented by four Hebrew letters, which in the Hebrew had no vowels with them. These four letters are called the Tetragrammaton and appear in English either as YHVH or YHWH. This name of God, sometimes called the Shem Hameforesh or the "Essence Name of the Creator," appears 6,823 times in the Holy Scriptures.

No one knows for sure how to pronounce YHVH or YHWH. One Hebrew source states that two vowels were given to one letter in the "Name," making it impossible to pronounce. Another source states that the vowel signs that had appeared above or below the consonants were replaced with the vowel signs for the Hebrew word Adonai by Jewish biblical scholars during the Middle Ages. This was in an effort to hide His "Name" to make certain it would not be taken in vain or blasphemed. Since Adonai means Lord in Hebrew, wherever the sacred Tetragrammaton appears in Scripture, today's Bible says LORD in all capital letters.

Dr. Danny Ben-Gigi, former department head of Hebrew studies at Arizona State University, says there is no way to know how YHVH or YHWH is pronounced. Some scholars maintain that it should be pronounced as Ye Ho Va H or Yehovah, which has been Anglicized to Jehovah. However, there is no J sound in Hebrew and, in fact, J was unknown in any alphabet until the 14th. century. Hence, Jehovah Jireh, as one of God's names is a poor transliteration.

Are there other names for God in the Bible?

The God of Abraham, Isaac and Jacob did not limit Himself to one name. For example:

Elohim is the only name for God in the first chapter of Genesis. Elohim is a masculine plural noun that emphasizes His majestic power and glory. Elohim is formed from the Hebrew word Alah (to swear) and describes One who is a covenant keeper.

El Shaddai means "Almighty God" and is found in Genesis 17:1. Shaddai comes from shad or breast, meaning the giver, pourer forth, or mother-like nature of God. El means might or power.

El Elyon means "Most High God" revealed in connection with Melchisedek in Genesis 14:18. This means the God in whom all things consist, the One in whom we live, and move and have our being.

Adonai means "Lord," and occurs approximately 300 times in the Tenach or the Old Testament. It is the plural of Adon, which means Lord or Master indicating a relationship like that of master/servant or husband/wife. He is the God who can be depended upon, trusted to sustain, to help and to keep.

Moses called God, YHVH Ne-See, the LORD our (victory) banner in Exodus 17:16. Gideon called God, YHVH Shalom, the LORD our Peace in Judges 6:24. David called God, YHVH Ro-ee, the LORD our Shepherd in Psalm

23:1. Jesus called God, Abba, which is a diminutive of the Aramaic word for Father and essentially means Daddy.

The word for JHVH or JHWH or Jehovah does not appear at all in the Greek text of the New Testament. Yes God revealed His name in the Old Testament as JHVH or JHWH, but in the New Testament, when we are given the spirit of adoption and brought into that intimate relationship as sons and daughters of God, we can look to Him and say Abba – Daddy.

What two chapters of the Bible are alike?

No two chapters of the Bible are exactly alike. However, there is very little difference between Isaiah 37 and II Kings 19. Isaiah 37 contains 38 verses while II Kings contains only 37 and there are other minor variations.

Large portions of Ezra 2 and Nehemiah 7 are also identical. Psalm 14 and Psalm 53 are substantially alike in matter, though not in form. Some of these duplications of parts of the Bible may have been owing to mistakes made by the early copyists of the manuscripts or to quotations that were not clearly indicated.

Similarities in Matthew, Mark and Luke are explained in a different manner. The authors of these synoptical gospels were telling essentially the same story and used many of the same sources. Matthew apparently borrowed from Mark, and Luke no doubt borrowed from both Matthew and Mark.

There are also many repetitions in Psalms. For instance, in Psalms 107 verses 8, 15, 21 and 31 are identical.

What caused the walls of Jericho to fall?

The taking of the fortified city of Jericho by the Israelites under Joshua is related in Joshua 6. What caused the walls of Jericho to fall is one of the biblical miracles that many attempt to explain as a natural phenomenon. Jericho lies in a region subject to numerous earth tremors and a favorite theory is that an earthquake shook down the walls of the heathen city.

Another theory, more ingenious, explains the phenomenon by what is known as synchronism. The notion is that the trumpet blasts and the shouts of the multitude, if in the proper rate of vibration, could have set up sufficient oscillation in the poorly constructed walls of Jericho and caused them to shake until they collapsed.

It is a fact that a comparatively small force, applied at regular intervals in favorable circumstances will occasionally set up considerable oscillation in suspension bridges. It has been said that a few soldiers marching over a long bridge in regular step might produce more vibration that a whole regiment out of step. That is why troops are generally ordered to route step before starting over a bridge. Two hundred and twenty-six men lost their lives in 1850 when a suspension bridge over the Marne at Angers, France, broke down on the 487 marching soldiers. The crash was caused by the vibration of the men in step combined with a great weight.

However, the theory that the walls of Jericho were shaking down by vibration caused by the trumpets and shouting is merely an interesting speculation. We know nothing about the construction of the walls of Jericho. It is supposed that Jericho fell to the Israelites about 1407 B.C., but a study of pottery, archeology, astronomy and history have shed little light on the Bible story. The authors of the Old Testament obviously believed in miracles, were not concerned with the scientific aspects of such problems, and they took it for granted that the collapse of the walls, when the trumpet sounded and the people shouted, was a miraculous intervention by God in behalf of the children of Israel.

How long is a Sabbath day's journey?

Under the Mosaic Law the Israelites were forbidden to travel on the Sabbath day (Exodus 16:29). It is evident, however, that the Israelites were permitted to go a certain distance on the Sabbath. For instance, they could go to the tabernacle or temple from the remote parts of the camp or city.

In the course of centuries the rabbinical authorities found ways, by legal fictions, to increase the distance that an Israelites might travel on the Sabbath day to make the restriction less burdensome. At first a Sabbath day's journey, the distance an Israelite might travel on the Sabbath from the wall limits of a town or city, was fixed at 2,000 cubits (Joshua 3:4-5). Later the rabbinical authorities interpreted place to mean town or city, so that an Israelite might travel 2,000 cubits outside the limits of his city on the Sabbath.

Still later the Pharisees doubled the length of the Sabbath day's journey by another legal fiction. They laid down the rule that if an Israelite deposited food at a definite place for the Sabbath he, by that act, made that figuratively the place of his abode and accordingly might travel 2,000 cubits further on the Sabbath, making a Sabbath day's journey 4,000 cubits.

What is the current equivalent of a Hebrew cubit?

It appears that the Hebrew cubit was a linear measure generally equivalent to 17.85 inches, although there is evidence that the Hebrew word so translated may sometimes refer to a measure equivalent to as much as 20 or more inches. The standards of measure in the Bible were long ago lost and it is very difficult to reproduce them. In later times the Jews adopted the measurements of the people who ruled them, or among whom they lived, while at the same time they retained the names of their own measurements that approximated them most nearly. Consequently the length of the Hebrew cubit probably varied at different times.

It is customary to assume, for convenience that the Hebrew cubit was 18 inches in length. Based on that assumption, the Sabbath day's journey of 4,000 cubits would have been

6,000 feet, a little over one mile. An English statute mile is 5,280 feet. In post Biblical times the Pharisees stretched the Sabbath day's journey again, making it 8,000 cubits, on the theory that a person, after going a distance of 4,000 cubits, would have to return.

There are few allusions to the Sabbath day's journey in the New Testament. In Acts 1:11 the distance from the Mount of Olives to Jerusalem is spoken of as a Sabbath day's journey. According to Josephus, the Mount of Olives was 6 furlongs, or about 3,495 feet from Jerusalem. Thus it would seem to the Sabbath day's journey in New Testament times was considerably less than one statute mile.

Under an old Puritan law in England it was permissible in the event of necessity to make a journey of 10 miles on Sunday. That distance, according to be medieval legal practice, was one half of an ordinary or weekday journey, namely, 20 miles.

Do the Jews practice baptism?

The baptism of converts in living water is of Jewish origin. Purification washings played an important part in the rites of the Hebrew religion from earliest times.

The fact that John the Baptist began his public ministry by baptizing in the Jordan appears to have attracted no special attention among the Jews. Yet the fact that he became known as "the Baptist" suggests that the kind of baptism he practiced was different from that generally prevalent in Judea.

While the Jews had baptized only Gentiles who became converts to Judaism, John baptized Jews as a symbol of their spiritual regeneration. His baptism apparently was performed on each individual only once in life and therefore differed from the periodic purification washings of the Jews. It symbolized a change in heart through repentance and a cleansing or rebirth proprietary to entrance into the Kingdom of God that the Baptist proclaimed as being near at hand.

The ancient Jewish right known as Jewish baptism or proselyte baptism naturally bears a striking similarity to Christian baptism, of which it was undoubtedly the forerunner, but it differed in significance. When a pagan became a convert to Judaism he was required, after submission to the Abrahamic right of circumcision, to go through a purification washing, which symbolized the removal of all pagan impurity. No stranger who sojourned among the Israelites could become completely one with them without complying with his rite of baptism.

Although Jews, as Christians understand it, do not practice baptism, today, Orthodox Jews still require the purification washings when Gentiles become converts to Judaism. But in Judaism it is circumcision rather than the rite of baptism that corresponds to Christian baptism as a symbol of conversion.

Have there been changes made in the King James Version of the Bible?

Evangelical Christianity has always maintained that the Holy Bible, in its original documents, is the infallible Word of God and forms the foundation of our faith. The King James translation of the Bible has served as an inspiration, not only to theologians, but to poets, dramatists, artists and politicians as well.

The Kings James Version of the Bible as it is published at the present time is not exact reprint of the first editions of 1611. Apparently the king's printers felt from the beginning that they were authorized to correct obvious errors and make minor changes in succeeding editions. As later editions were printed typographical errors were corrected, spelling and punctuation were altered and modernized, and italics and capital letters were varied. These alterations were made so gradually that it is difficult to say just who made them.

When the King James Version first appeared in 1611 it contained a notice to the readers, a calendar and the Apocrypha. All these have been eliminated from most modern editions.

At the time the first edition was issued the letters J and I on the one hand, and letters V and U on the other where not differentiated. Jesus was printed Iesus, and Joseph was printed Ioseph. Heaven was printed Heauen, and upon was printed vpon. In some cases, the old f-shaped or long s was used in the original edition.

According to the original editions, I Corinthians 12:28 read, "And God hath set some in the church, first apostles, secondarily prophets, thirdly teachers, after that miracles, then gifts of healings, helps in governments, diversities of tongues." Helps in governments was obviously a misprint. After running through several successive editions this was corrected and "helps, governments" was substituted. But on whose authority this justified change was made is hard to say.

In the first of other two editions issued in 1611, the last clause in Ruth was printed, "And *he* went into the city Consequently, this edition is sometimes known as the "He Bible," or the "Great He Bible." In the second edition of 1611 the passage in Ruth was changed to read, "And *she* went into the city," and that reading has been retained to this day. That edition is known as the "She Bible." Oddly enough, *he* is the correct translation of the Hebrew original.

What is the Revised Version of the Bible?

The revised Version is a liberal revision of the King James Version. In 1870, in response to a widespread demand for an up to date version of the English Bible, both convocations of the Anglican Church adopted a resolution calling for such a revision. The plan was to preserve the unsurpassed English of the King James Version and at the same time modernize its language and correct its inaccuracies in the light of modern scholarship.

Seventy-five Anglo American scholars, divided into Old and New Testament groups in both England and America, did the work. About 36,000 major and minor changes in the English of the King James Version were made. The Revised New Testament was published in 1881, the Revised Old Testament in 1885, and the Revised Apocrypha in 1895.

In some cases beauty of style was sacrificed for accuracy and in others stilted Latinisms were substituted for time-honored English phraseology. Because many of the changes were not acceptable to English speaking Protestants, the Revised Version has never supplanted the King James Version. The American groups continued their work and in 1901 published the American Standard or the American Revised Version. These revised versions are now dated in their English, as is the older version on which they were based.

Although there are many archaic words in the King James Version, it contains comparatively few obsolete words. This is because the revisers and translators of the version of 1611 were careful to choose words already firmly fixed in the language and because the popularity of the work has had a tendency to keep alive all words in it.

How large is the vocabulary of the English Bible?

The vocabulary of the English Bible is small compared to the total number of words in the English language. It is generally estimated that the total number of different words, exclusive of proper names, in the King James Version is only about 7,000, 5,642 of which are in the Old Testament.

Naturally a vocabulary cannot be numbered with mathematical accuracy because authorities differ as to just what is regarded as a separate word. For instance, one authority will consider "work" and "worked" as two words, while another will reckon them as one word. Consequently estimates of the size of the vocabulary of the English Bible range from 7000 to 10,000 words.

How did the saying "poor as Job's turkey" originate?

The older phrase "patient as Job" apparently suggested "poor as Job's turkey." In James 5:11 it is said that, "Indeed we count them blessed who endure. You have heard of the perseverance of Job." This of course refers to the patriarch whose history is related in The Book of Job and whose patience is proverbial.

Some writers suppose that "poor as Job's turkey" was originated by Thomas Chandler Haliburton in The Clockmaker, or The Sayings and Doings of Samuel Slick of Slickville. Haliburton, a native of Nova Scotia was a Canadian humorist and historian. He described a turkey gobbler that was so poor that he had only one feather in his tail and so weak that he had to lean against the fence to gobble. This condition was attributed to the gobbler's persistent efforts to hatch chicks from eggs that did not have chicks in them.

Turkey was probably associated with Job in phrases before the Sam Slick stories appeared in 1837. In 1824 the Sentinel of Troy, New York, quoted the following extract from a paper called the Microscope, "We have seen fit to say the *patience of Job's turkey*, instead of the common phrase, *as patient as Job*. And so it must go for this time at any rate."

Although turkey is of Old World origin, Job could not have had a bird of the species we call turkey, because this branch of pheasant family was native to America. In the New Testament Job is mentioned by name only in James 5:11 as quoted above, but The Book of Job is quoted in I Corinthians 3:19 which says in part, "He catches the wise in their own craftiness," which is taken from Job 5:13.

Why do we call the Scriptures the Bible?

Bible as the name of the Jewish-Christian sacred writings as a whole is a comparatively new term. This term would have meant nothing to a Jew in the time of Jesus. In those days the Hebrew Scriptures were thought of not as one book but as many books.

The canonization of the Old Testament was a gradual process that was not completed until 40 or 50 years after the crucifixion Jesus. At that time the Jews divided their sacred writings into three grand divisions: The Law which are the first five books of Moses; The Prophets which are Joshua, Judges, Samuel, Kings, Isaiah, Jeremiah, Ezekiel, and the 12 minor prophets; and The Writings which are the rest of the Old Testament sacred books. Since Jesus referred to the sacred writings as only "the law and the prophets" some theologians have concluded that the writings were not yet canonized.

The word Bible comes to us from ancient Egypt by way of Greece, Italy and France. Biblios was the Greek name for the inner bark of the Egyptian papyrus reed, the material from which paper was first made and on which books were written in New Testament times. In time biblios came to signify not only paper but a book, roll or scroll in general. The diminutive of biblios is biblion, and the plural of biblion is biblia, meaning "little books."

However, at an early date the singular and plural were used interchangeably. For example, in the Greek of Matthew 1:1 biblios occurs in "the book of generations," while in the Greek of Luke 4:17 biblion occurs in "the book of the prophet Esaias." The Latins borrowed this word, transcribed it biblia and treated as a singular. In I Maccabees, which is regarded as canonical by Catholics and Apocryphal by Protestants, biblia is employed in reference to the Hebrew sacred writings.

John Chrysostom, patriarch of Constantinople, in the fourth century A.D. referred to the general collection of Jewish and Christian writings as biblia, "the books," but which was probably construed as a singular. It was not until the 13th century that the English form Bible occurred as the name of the Old and New Testament, and even then it was used in the general sense of "the book" or the "book of books."

Chauncer, writing in the 14th century, continued to use the term in the sense of any book, and its original meaning is retained in such compounds as bibliography (a list of books), bibliophile (a lover of books) and bibliopole (a seller of books). In the million plus words attributed to Shakespeare, the word Bible does not appear once. The words Holy Writ, Scripture, Scriptures, Gospel and similar terms do. The word Bible is not used in either the text or in the Epistle Dedicatory of the King James Version of the Bible.

The Jews had generally referred to their sacred writings by a name meaning the books. The New Testament writers referred to them by the Greek hai graphia meaning the writings. In Latin this became scripturae from which we get our word scriptures. It came to be applied to the Bible without qualification because that book or collection of books was looked upon as "the writings."

The same is true of the Koran, the name of the Moslem sacred writings. The word Koran comes from an Arabic word signifying to read.

Do Moslems believe in the exclusivity of their religion?

It is important to understand that Christianity is not the only religion that claims exclusivity. Muslims radically claim exclusivity as well. They do so not just theologically but linguistically as well. Muslims believe that the sole, sufficient, and consummate miracle of Islam is the Qur'an and that it is only recognizable in Arabic. Any other translation "desacralizes" it. The Qur'an itself acknowledges that if it contains any errors anywhere, it did not come from God (Sura 4, "Women," verse 82).

Do Moslems believe in the Old and New Testaments of the Bible?

Muhammad based his teachings largely upon the Old and New Testaments, upon Arabic tradition and upon his own philosophy. It is generally supposed that Muhammad obtained his knowledge of the Scriptures orally (since he could not read) by conversing with Arabic Jews and Christians. The Bible plays a very minor role in Islam. Moslem authorities hold that wherever the Qur'an differs from the Bible, the Jews and Christians have corrupted or perverted the Biblical text.

Moslems recognize six prophets: Adam, Noah, Abraham, Moses, Jesus and Muhammad. Muhammad regarded himself as the successor of Jesus and the last of the prophets. Of the other five prophets of Islam, Abraham and Jesus are regarded as the principal ones. Islam, like Judaism, is a strictly monotheistic religion, and Moslems do not worship Muhammad or any of the other prophets as a deity. The essence of Islam is, "There is only one God, Allah, and Muhammad is his prophet." Consequently, the Moslems, while they accept Jesus as one of the six prophets, do not worship Him or hold to a triune God as Christians do. Moslems, like the Gnostics (erroneously in my personal opinion), believe that Jesus was not Himself crucified but another (perhaps even Judas) in His likeness. Jesus, according to the Qur'an, was taken unharmed directly to heaven (Sura 3, "The Imrans," verse 55 and Sura 4, "Women," verses 156-158.)

What do Moslems teach about the Christian Trinity?

It is true that the Qur'an affirms that Jesus was the Jewish Messiah and a true prophet of God, that he was virgin born and performed many miracles. Therefore, Moslems believe, because the Qur'an teaches these very true and proper things about Jesus, that Christians should be laudatory of them and look upon them as supportive of Christian beliefs.

However, a careful reading of the Qur'an will disclose that Muhammad did not have a clear grasp of what classic orthodox Christianity was teaching about the Trinity in the seventh century A.D. He was hearing views that had been totally rejected by the early fathers of the church. Muhammad's consistent representation of the Trinity suggests that he conceived the idea of a trinity along the lines of crude tri-theism, a heresy that Christianity had consistently repudiated. In Sura 5, "The Table," verse 116, he teaches that Christians believe that God's "three-ness" is composed of Allah, Jesus (whom he believed ill-informed Christians had wrongly deified), and Jesus' mother Mary.

Now whatever sub-scriptural oddities some church fathers may have espoused over the early centuries of the church about God as Trinity, I can declare categorically that not one of them ever taught that God's "three-ness" included the mother of Jesus, nor has any ecumenical council ever endorsed such a notion. There was a fourth century heretical sect made up of fanatical women called Collyridians existing in Arabia that had rendered divine worship to Mary and perhaps it was the existence of this sect that gave Muhammad the false impression that Christians thought Mary was a member of the divine Triad.

In any case, this is an error of massive proportions on Muhammad's part and shows ignorance of Christian teaching. It also shows that the Qur'an contains a significant error respecting this major doctrine in the belief system of one of its major religious contenders. Christianity has historically declared in its creeds and confessions that within the unity of the one living and true God eternally exist three persons: God the Father, God the Son, and God the Holy Spirit; that these three are one God, the same in substance and equal in power and glory.

Why are the two parts of the Bible called testaments?

Testament, from the Latin *testamentum*, is used in the English New Testament to render the Greek *diatheke*, which signifies primarily "a disposition of property by will" and sometimes "a compact, agreement or covenant." The phrases Old Testament and New Testament both occur in the King James Version, where they are used in a general rather than in a specific sense.

At the Last Supper, Matthew 26:28 records Jesus saying, "This is my blood of the new testament." The same phrase is found in corresponding passages in Mark 14:24 and Luke 22:20. In Second Corinthians, chapter 3, Paul refers to the New Testament in verse 6 and to the Old Testament in verse 14. In Hebrews 9:15-20 the term testament is used in both its primary and secondary meanings.

The Israelites referred to the compact made between God and His chosen people as *Berith*, which is rendered covenant in the English version of the Old Testament. However, the Israelites never conceived the sacred books themselves as a single covenant, will or testament. The Jewish religion was based on a series of covenants (Adamic, Noahic, Abrahamic, Mosaic and Davidic) between God and His people. In Christianity, Calvinists embrace covenant theology which includes the above five Jewish covenants plus a sixth, the new covenant. These covenants are not seen as distinct or separate, but rather that each covenant builds on the previous one, culminating in the new covenant, yielding one overall major covenant, know as the covenant of grace.

To the Jews in the time of Jesus the idea of an Old Testament would have been incomprehensible. Even for several generations after the crucifixion of Jesus, Christians and Jews alike continued to use the same Bible. At first the Christians did not think of their early writings as parts of the Scriptures. None of the New Testament books were consciously written for a place in the "New Testament."

However, most if not all of the New Testament writings had been completed and were in possession of the churches by the second century, and gradually Christians began to place these writings on an equal footing with the Hebrew Bible. It was not till then that Christians began to think in terms of the Old and New Testaments as the sacred writings that made up the Bible of the Church.

At the council of Carthage in 397 A. D. the canon of the New Testament was fixed substantially in its present form. The Old Testament covers a period of history extending from creation to about 400 B.C.; while the New Testament covers a period of only about seventy years, from shortly before the birth of Jesus until shortly before the death of Paul at the time of Nero.

Did the English Bible originally contain the letter J?

"J" in English is a comparatively late variant of the Latin "I" and was not regarded as a separate letter in the alphabet at the time the King James Version of the Bible was printed. In Alexander Cruden's famous <u>Concordance of the Bible</u> in 1737, words beginning with "I" and "J' are printed under "I" as if they were the same letter. The letters were not entirely differentiated until the nineteenth century.

Colonel Charles K. Gardner, the author of the system of using letters to designate companies in the U. S. Army, omitted the letter "J" to avoid confusion, because when the system was established in 1816 "I" and "J" were often written exactly alike. For the same reason there was no "J" street in Washington, D. C.

Does any verse in the Bible contain all the letters of the alphabet?

Ezra 7:21 is often cited as a Bible verse containing all the letters of the English alphabet, but this verse does not contain "J," a fact that indicates that this verse was first pointed out for this distinction before "J" and "I" were differentiated. This same fact explains why the Christian symbol *JHS* is also written *IHS*. This symbol is from the Latin, *Iesus* (or *Jesus), Hominum Salvator*, for "Jesus, the Savior of Men."

What is the Gideon Bible?

The Gideon Bible is not a version of the Bible, but merely the popular name for Bibles distributed by *The Gideons*, an association of Christian businessmen who are in good standing as members of a church or religious society. The Gideons were organized on July 1, 1899. It is a non-denominational association and according to its original declaration, its purpose is to band together Christian travelers and through them: win business travelers for the glory of God; supply every hotel in America with a Bible in each guest room; and prepare the hearts of travelers for salvation.

The name Gideon is taken from one of the judges of Israel whose history is related in the book of Judges, chapters 6 and 7. A pitcher with a lamp inside of it is the emblem of the Gideons, in allusion to the pitchers and lamps carried by Gideon and his three hundred followers when the Midianites were delivered into their hands.

Funds for purchasing the Bibles that they distribute are raised by members in their local churches. The work of the Gideons is done gratis and those performing it are not permitted to use any of the money collected for personal expenses. Money paid as dues and contributions by the regular and associate members of the society are used for that purpose. Local units of the Gideons are called Camps.

When was the first Bible printed and by whom?

As far as can be estimated Johannes Gutenberg began cutting type around 1450. Composition began in 1452, and the printing was completed by 1456. The most reliable estimate suggests that, as few as 185 copies were produced, of which about 40 copies still exist today.

The Gutenberg Bible was in Latin, the language of the Church, of scholarship and of diplomacy. The first translation of the Bible into the living languages of Western Europe was in German, about ten years later in 1466, and was printed by Mentelin of Strasbough. William Tyndale published the first edition of the English New Testament in Wroms in 1526. The first complete English Bible appeared in 1535. This was the work of Miles Coverdale.

What is the relation of Sabaoth to Sabbath?

Sabaoth (SABB-a-oath or so-BAY-oath) occurs only twice in the King James as well as in the New King James Versions of the Bible, both times in the New Testament, and it is a Hebrew word meaning "armies" or "hosts." It has no relation to Sabbath, which literally means "rest."

For some reason the English translators saw fit to let Sabaoth remain un-translated in Romans 9:29 and James 5:4. In other parts of the Bible the Hebrew form of Jehovah Sabaoth is rendered by "the Lord of Hosts" or an equivalent English phrase. Martin Luther uses the term in his great Reformation hymn, "A Mighty Fortress is Our God," where in the second stanza he writes, "Christ Jesus it is He, Lord Sabaoth His name."

Sabaoth is often confused with Sabbath and has been so confused by many noted writers in the past. Edmund Spenser in the last stanza of the "Faerie Queen" confuses the terms, as did Shakespeare in the second folio of The Merchant of Venice. Dr. Samuel Johnson treated the two words as if they were identical in the first edition of his dictionary and Sir Walter Scott in Ivanhoe erroneously refers to "the grains of a week, aye the space between two Sabaoths."

What does Mizpah mean?

Mizpah is a Hebrew word literally meaning, "watch tower." Originally it was applied to places where a watch or garrison was maintained and it became the name of several towns and places in ancient Palestine. The term in the Hebrew Bible is spelled both Mizpah and Mizpeh, without any difference in meaning; BUT when spelled Mizpah it is invariably preceded by the definite article (the Mizpah) except in Hosea 5:1.

The name is particularly applied to the pillar set up and the heap of stones gathered on Mt. Gilead by Jacob and his brethren as a witness of the covenant made there with Laban. In modern usage Mizpah or the Mizpah Benediction signifies a parting salutation, a meaning suggested by Genesis 31:49, which contains Laban's prayer at Mizpah, "May the Lord watch between you and me when we are absent one from another." The context, however, indicates that Laban's words were more in the nature of a mutual warning than a blessing.

Do you agree that most worship services should no longer include a recitation of either Apostles' or Nicene Creed?

While I have never held any brief for vain repetitions in worship services, I believe anticreedalism in this country has significantly harmed Protestantism and evangelicalism. It has paved the way for a new liberalism based on an ignorance of Biblical facts, and not a rejection of them.

The removal of these great historic creeds and the explanations of them in many of our church worship services have, in my opinion, watered down the understanding of the Gospel to a point where it has almost dissipated into total existentialism, an experientialism based on feelings alone. There cannot be a world wide missionary vision without the Gospel, and there will be no Gospel to preach without agreement as to what we should teach. We need to return to our

Christian roots and the Gospel as best summed up in these creeds.

Should contemporary Christian music be part of a worship service?

At a given time in history, any piece of music (including the singing of psalms and Gregorian chants) found in Christian worship services today was considered contemporary. If the church from its inception had excluded contemporary music from the worship service, we would find little or no music in the church today. Therefore, the answer to the question is yes, but with the following caveat.

We should not make a broad judgment about the worship worthiness of Christian music solely on the basis of whether it is contemporary or traditional. I find much, but not all, of contemporary music simplistic, vainly repetitive, subjective (self focused), emotive, and very poor theologically and thus should not be part of worship. Of course, there are some traditional hymns of which these same criticisms may appropriately be made.

The object of our worship is God almighty and not our subjective selves. It is He that is worthy. The main purpose of our reading, praying and singing (either contemporary or traditional music), indeed all the acts of our worship, must be to focus on His worthiness alone. If we are focused on whether we are singing contemporary songs or traditional hymns when we are in worship, then our focus is not where it ought to be. The ineffable glory of the great and majestic God whom we serve calls for our full attention and the best efforts of our hearts, minds and voices. Nothing less will do.

What is the Jefferson Bible?

The Jefferson Bible is a compilation made by Thomas Jefferson and consists of passages from the four gospels cut out and pasted a book according to a scheme of his own. Before beginning the work, Jefferson tried to get Dr. Benjamin Rush to compile such a work. He sent Dr. Rush a comparative outline of the moral teachings of Jesus and those of certain ancient philosophers, and explained to his friend why his name should not be associated with the enterprise.

During his early political campaigns Jefferson had been widely denounced as an atheist and an unbeliever because he showed little interest in formal and conventional church work. So the man who was the author of the Statute for Religious Freedom in Virginia and who more than any other was responsible for the provision in the Bill of Rights guaranteeing to Americans the free exercise of religion, wrote to Dr. Rush as follows:

> And in confiding it to you, I know it will not be exposed to the malignant perversions of those who make every word from me a text for new misrepresentations and calumnies (slander). I am, moreover, adverse to the communication of my religious tenets to the public, because it would countenance the presumption of those who have endeavored to draw them before that tribunal, and to seduce public opinion to erect itself into that inquest over the rights of conscience, which the laws have so justly proscribed. It behooves everyman who values liberty of conscience for himself to resist invasions of it in the case of others, or their case may, by change of circumstances, become his own.

Unable to get another to do it, Jefferson, then serving his first term as President of the United States, began the work in 1804. He bought two copies of the English Bible and spent two evenings at home in the White House cutting out and pasting into a blank book the words attributed to Jesus and some other passages in close accord with the words of the great teacher. This work he found an agreeable and profitable escape from the affairs of state. He thought this first abridgement (digest or abstract) might be adapted for the use of the Indians.

We learn from a letter to a friend that Jefferson was in the habit of reading from this volume every night before going to bed. In 1813 he wrote from Monticello to John Adams: "We must reduce our volume to the simple Evangelists; select, even from them, the very words only of Jesus, paring off the amphibologisms (ambiguous) into which they have been led, by forgetting often, or not understanding, what had fallen from Him, by giving their own misconceptions as His dicta, and expressing unintelligibly for others what they had not understood themselves. There will be found remaining the most sublime and benevolent code of morals which has ever been offered to man. I have performed this operation for my own use, cutting verse by verse out of the printed book, and arranging the matter which is evidently His and which is as easy distinguished as diamonds in a dunghill. The result is an octave of forty-six pages."

In 1816 Jefferson wrote to Charles Thomson: "I, too, have made a wee little book from the same materials, which I call the philosophy of Jesus; it is a paradigma (model) of His doctrines, made by cutting the texts out of the book, arranging them on the pages of a blank book, in a certain order of time and subject. A more beautiful or precious morsel of ethics I have never seen; it is a document in proof that I am a real Christian, that is to say a disciple of the doctrines of Jesus." Jefferson in his letter to Thomson added; "If I had time I would add to my little book the Greek, Latin and French texts, in columns side-by-side."

About 1819 Jefferson found the time to complete the work by cutting out and pasting in parallel columns in a blank book the corresponding passages from New Testaments in Greek, Latin and French, three languages that Jefferson read with ease. The finished work he entitled *The Life and Morals of Jesus of Nazareth*. There are no notes or commentaries in the book except the section of the Roman law under which Jesus was brought to trial. The lists of passages, the title pages and references are in Jefferson's handwriting. Two maps, one of Palestine and another of the ancient world are pasted in front. Jefferson never published his Bible. "I not only write nothing on religion," he said, "but rarely permit myself to speak on it."

In 1895 the Federal Government purchased this curious book from the Jefferson heirs and the original is now in the National Museum at Washington. Nine years later the Fifty-seventh Congress issued a limited edition of the English section of the Jefferson Bible for distribution to its members. Since then this interesting work, compiled in the White House by a President of the United States, has been printed by private publishers and is available to the public.

What are the longest and shortest chapters in the Bible?

Both the shortest and the longest chapters of the Bible are found in the Book of Psalms. Psalm 117 has the distinction of being the shortest as well as the middle chapter in the Bible. Psalm 119, which has 176 verses, is the longest.

Psalm 119 is an acrostic, or alphabetic, psalm of twenty-two stanzas, each beginning sequentially with a letter of the Hebrew alphabet. The eight poetic lines of each stanza begins with the same Hebrew letter. Other acrostic psalms are 9-10, 25, 34, 37, 111, 112, 119 and 145.

Are not *Ethics* and *Morals* the same thing?

Although the term ethics is often used interchangeably with morals or morality, historically the two have had very different meanings. Ethics (from the Greek ethos) conveyed the sense of a dwelling place, a place of stability and permanence. Morality (from the word mores) describes the behavioral pattern of a given society.

Ethics is a normative science in that it prescribes what should be. Morality is a descriptive science in that it indicates what is. Ethics are absolute while morals are relative.

Consequently, when morality and ethics are used interchangeably, as we do in today's post-modern society, the normal (what is) becomes the normative (what should be). Good is determined by the normal or the statistical average. There is an obvious fault in making a "what is" into a "what should be."

Conformity to a given society's self-established norm then becomes the ethical obligation instead of conformity to externally imposed imperatives by a Sovereign God. For believers, this means being called to non-conformity (with regard to many of the "accepted morals" in our society), to a transforming ethic that shatters the normal, that shatters the "what is." Biblical ethics is obedience to God.

Is war ethical?

There are three possible positions an individual may take regarding war; these are activism, pacifism or select-ism. Activism views all wars as permissible. Pacifism views all wars, and hence ones involvement in them, as wrong. Select-ism views war as wrong, but one's involvement in a war may be justifiable. It is from this third position that the "just war" theory has emerged in Christian history. Select-ism argues that the victim nation of a clear-cut act of aggression has the right of self-defense

Francis Hopkinson (a signer of the Declaration of Independence) defined war, in his "A Political Catechism" written in 1777, as the curse of mankind, the foundation of which "is laid in the wickedness of mankind." He divided war into offensive and defensive wars and stated that a defensive war was not only justifiable but an indispensable duty. "Otherwise," Hopkinson said, "a few miscreants (unprincipled individuals) would tyrannize over the rest of mankind and make the passive multitude the slaves of their power."

Was the war with Iraq a just war since Iraq did not attack our borders?

Francis Hopkinson defined a defensive war as one in which a nation takes up "arms in opposition to the invasion of usurped dangers, to secure the rights of humanity and the blessings of freedom, to generations yet unborn." Hopkinson, writing in 1777, did not delimit an "immediate invasion" to a physical attack on one's borders. Dr. Robert P. George, ethics professor at Princeton University writes, "Preemptive action is 'defensive' when it is motivated by a reasonable belief that a proven aggressor is in the process of equipping himself with the military means to carry out further aggression with impunity."

Iraq attacked Iran in 1980 and Kuwait in 1990. It launched ballistic missiles against several surrounding nations. Its leader, Saddam Hussein, ordered the death of people in Kurdish villages, and gassed Iranians as well as citizens in his own country. From this, as well as by the number of violated UN resolutions, we may conclude that Saddam Hussein is a proven aggressor. While few want war, even a justifiable one, I would note that Jesus never told a member of the military not to perform his or her duty.

Has the United States Congress ever endorsed the Bible?

One year after the signing of the Declaration of Independence, America had a shortage of several imported commodities, including Bibles. On September 11, 1777 Congress ordered 20,000 Bibles to be imported from Holland, Scotland and other places "into the different ports of the States of the Union." As the war for independence prolonged the shortage of Bibles grew. In 1781, Congress approved a request from Robert Aitken, the publisher of *The Pennsylvania Magazine*, to print Bibles in America rather than import them.

On September 12, 1782, Congress approved that Bible, the first English Bible ever printed in America. The first page of that Bible contained this Congressional endorsement, "Resolved: That the United States in Congress assembled . . . recommend this edition of the Bible to the inhabitants of the United States."

What does the Bible say about spiritual mediums?

A list of prohibited occult practices is given in Deuteronomy 18:10-11. Included is "a medium, or a spiritualist, or one who consults the dead." Such a practice is not allowed in the New Testament and converts who had previously practiced such, burnt their textbooks (Acts 19:19).

In First Samuel 28 we read that after the death of Samuel, Saul disguised himself and sought out a medium. Such mediums were outlawed in Israel and such activity was a capital offense. Not only was it a capital offense under Mosaic Law (Leviticus 20:27), but also Saul himself had enforced this and insisted that all such mediums who consulted the dead leave the land. That is why Saul disguised himself. We cannot be sure whether the Bible is speaking in phenomenological language or whether the medium was in fact able to bring Samuel back from the dead.

We can say for sure that if the dead can be contacted, those of us who believe in God are not allowed to do so. There is no question about that. Scripture is clear that the use of mediums is anathema to God and people who do use mediums are included in the final chapter of the New Testament (Revelation 22:15) as those who are excluded from the Kingdom of God.

Can one converse in Hebrew?

Like Aramaic and Greek, the other two original languages of the Scriptures, Hebrew is a dead language in its ancient form. Because of the limited vocabulary it would be impossible for anyone to carry on a satisfactory conversation on current topics in pure Hebrew.

But Hebrew has continued to be a sacred, literary and ritual language among the Jews, and after World War I it was revived in a modernized form. Hebrew, with an enlarged vocabulary from other languages, and not Yiddish, is regarded as the national language in Israel.

Aramaic in its ancient form is a dead language, but dialects closely akin to it are still spoken by the Samaritans in the Mediterranean region. Greek is the ritual language in some Eastern Orthodox churches.

Are there any original Biblical manuscripts in existence?

There are no original manuscripts of the Bible in existence. The oldest known Biblical manuscripts are copies, not originals. Probably in the case of most books of the Bible there never were original copies "handwritten" by the authors. We are told in Jeremiah 36 that the prophet dictated his book to Baruch. That was the usual custom of writers in ancient times.

Even the first two copies of the Epistles of Paul were not autographs of the Apostle Paul. Paul was in the habit of dictating the body of his letters to a secretary and of then adding a salutation or a few words in his own hand so his correspondents would know them to be authentic. In First Corinthians 16:21 he says, "The salutation with my own hand," and in Second Thessalonians 3:17, "The salutation of Paul with my own hand, which is a sign in every epistle; so I write." In Romans 16:22 Paul's amanuensis or secretary identifies himself, "I, Tertius, who wrote this epistle, greet you in the Lord." It is probable that virtually all the books of the Bible were dictated to scribes by their authors.

My King James Bible says it was translated from the original languages, so doesn't that mean the translators used original manuscripts?

There are no known first or original copies of the books of the Bible in existence. When the authors of the King James Version said they "translated out of the original languages," they did not mean they had access to "original manuscripts," but rather that they consulted copies in Hebrew, Greek and perhaps other ancient languages instead of merely relying upon previous translations. The date when a Bible book was completed and the date of the oldest copy of that book are two entirely different matters.

What is the oldest city in the world?

It is generally supposed that Damascus, the chief city of Syria, is the oldest city in the world. Although positive evidence is wanting, there is some reason for believing that its site has been occupied longer and more continuously as a city than any other spot on earth.

The Jewish historian Josephus, who probably based his assertion on Hebrew tradition, attributed the foundation of Damascus to Uz, the son of Aram and great grandson of Noah. In Genesis 14 it is related that Abraham pursued the routed kings to Hobah, "which is north of Damascus" (verse 15). This is evidence that Damascus was already a place of importance in the time of Abraham, who lived two thousand years or more before Christ. Damascus and the part of Syria, of which it was the capital, was placed under tribute to the Israelites under David.

Why do we clasp our hands in prayer?

Clasping the hands in prayer is merely a conventional form of holding up the hands toward heaven. The earliest imitation of a posture assumed by the Israelites during prayer is found in Exodus 17, where Moses held up his hands during a battle between his people and Amalek. We first read of the offering of sacrifice and prayer being associated in Leviticus 9:22, "Then Aaron lifted his hand toward the people, blessed them, and came down from offering the sin offering, the burnt offering, and peace offerings."

Psalm 141:2 says, "Let my prayer be set before You as incense, The lifting up of my hands as the evening sacrifice," and 143:6, "I spread out my hands to You." In Nehemiah 8:6 we read, "And Ezra blessed the Lord, the great God. Then all the people answered, 'Amen, Amen!' while lifting up their hands. And they bowed their heads and worshiped the Lord with their faces to the ground."

Stretching out the hands seems to be a natural attitude assumed by inferiors when asking favors of, presenting petitions or doing homage to, superiors and is apparently one of the primitive instincts of the human race. However, no particular posture of prayer is prescribed in the Bible. The bodily attitudes assumed during prayer are standing, sitting, kneeling, bowing toward the ground and prostrating oneself. All these positions imply humility, respect and reverence.

Isaac Disraeli, in <u>Curiosities of Literature</u>, wrote: "To bend and prostrate one's self to express sentiments of respect appears to be a natural motion; for terrified persons throw themselves on the earth when they adore invisible beings." According to First Samuel 1:26, Hannah, the mother of Samuel, stood when she prayed to the Lord, and First Kings 8:22 says, "Then Solomon stood before the altar of the Lord in the presence of all the assembly of Israel, and spread out his hands toward heaven." In the parable of the Pharisee and the publican, who went into the temple to pray, both stood, but the publican would not even lift his eyes to heaven but struck his breast. Second Samuel 7:18 tell us that David sat before the Lord when he prayed.

Kneeling, bowing the head and prostrating the body were gestures of honor and respect as well as of worship and prayer. Genesis 43:26 says Joseph's brothers bowed down and made obeisance to their brother. When Joseph rode in Pharaoh's chariot they cried out before him to bend the knee. Isaiah 45:23 says, "That to Me every knee shall bow." In Genesis 24:26 we are told that the man bowed his head and worshipped the Lord. "Oh come, let us worship and bow down; Let us kneel before the Lord our Maker," says Psalm 95:6. According to Daniel 6:10, Daniel kneeled three times a day and prayed. Ezra, in Ezra 9:5 says, "I fell on my knees and spread out my hands to the Lord my God." Jesus, in Luke 22:41, kneeled down and prayed and Acts 7:60 says Stephen kneeled down. Luke 17:16 tells us that the Samaritan leper who had been healed fell on his face at the feet of Jesus and gave Him thanks.

Does the Bible call the Israelites the chosen people?

The specific phrase, "the chosen people," is not in the Bible, but it is strongly suggested by various Bible passages. According to First Chronicles 16:13, David sang a psalm in which he said, "O seed of Israel His servant, You children of Jacob, His chosen ones!" Psalm 33:12 says, "Blessed is the nation whose God is the Lord, The people He has chosen as His own inheritance." Verse 6 of Psalm 105 says, "O seed of Abraham His servant, You children of Jacob, His chosen ones!" Verse 43 of the same Psalm says, "He brought out His people with joy, His chosen ones with gladness." First Chronicles 16:13 says, "O seed of Israel His servant, You children of Jacob, His chosen ones!"

The same thought is expressed in the New Testament. In Acts 13:17, Paul says, "The God of this people Israel chose our fathers, and exalted the people when they dwelt as strangers in the land of Egypt."

How many tribes of Israel were there?

It is commonly supposed that the tribes of Israel were all named after sons of Jacob and that they numbered twelve. That is not quite correct.

There were really thirteen instead of twelve. Jacob, who was called Israel, had twelve sons by his two wives and his two concubines, Leah, Rachel, Zilpah and Bilhah. The names of the twelve sons were: Reuben, Simeon, Levi, Judah, Issachar, Zebulon, Gad, Asher, Dan, Naphtali, Joseph and Benjamin.

According to Genesis 49:28, after Jacob had blessed all of his twelve sons in succession, he said, "All these are the twelve tribes of Israel, and this is what their father spoke to them. And he blessed them; he blessed each one according to his own blessing." But Jacob had already indicated that no tribe would bear Joseph's name. By Asenath, daughter of an Egyptian priest, Joseph had two sons. In Genesis 48:5-6 Jacob said to Joseph, "And now your two sons, Ephraim and Manasseh, who were born to you in the land of Egypt before I came to you in Egypt, are mine; as Reuben and Simeon, they shall be mine. Your offspring whom you beget after them shall be yours; they will be called by the name of their brothers in their inheritance." Consequently there were really thirteen tribes, eleven named after sons and two after grandsons of Jacob.

When the Israelites settled in the Promised Land only twelve tribes were allotted separate territory. The tribe of Levi was consecrated as a tribe of hereditary priests and they were assigned dwelling privileges in forty-eight cities scattered in the territory allotted to the other twelve tribes. Nevertheless the Levites continued to be referred to as the tribe of Levi.

Twelve was a sacred number among the ancient Hebrews and when the tribe of Levi was withdrawn as a separate political and military unit, an additional tribe was created by subdividing the tribe of Joseph into Ephraim and Manasseh. This respect for the number twelve apparently survived among the Jews down to New Testament times. Jesus had twelve disciples, but after Judas Iscariot betrayed his master and committed suicide, the remaining eleven chose a successor, Matthias. In Acts 1:26 we are told, "And they cast their lots, and the lot fell on Matthias. And he was numbered with the eleven apostles." While Judas was still in apparent good standing, Jesus, in Matthew 19:28, said to his disciples, "Assuredly I say to you, that in the regeneration, when the Son of Man sits on the throne of His glory, you who have followed Me will also sit on twelve thrones, judging the twelve tribes of Israel."

What was "the river of Egypt"?

The "river of Egypt" mentioned several times in the Old Testament was not the Nile as popularly supposed. According to Genesis 15:18, "On the same day the Lord made a covenant with Abram, saying: "To your descendants I have given this land, from the river of Egypt to the great river, the River Euphrates." In Number 34:5 the Lord, speaking to Moses about the boundaries of the Promised Land, says, "And the border shall fetch a compass from Azmon unto the river of Egypt, and the goings out of it shall be at the sea."

This "river of Egypt" has been identified with the broad and shallow watercourse known to the modern Arabs as the Wady el-'Arish, which runs north and northwest from the Sinaitic peninsula and flows into the Mediterranean about fifty miles southwest of Gaza. It is a typical *wadi* or "flash stream," being virtually dry except during the rainy season, when it becomes a swift river. First Kings 8:65 says, "And at that time Solomon held a feast, and all Israel with him, a great congregation, from the entering in of Hamath unto the river of Egypt." This "river of Egypt" was regarded by the Israelites as the border of Egypt and the southern boundary of Solomon's kingdom.

The Nile is nowhere mentioned by that name in the King James Version of the Bible. Nile is the Anglicized form of the classical name of this great river. The Egyptians never knew it by that name and there is no corresponding word for it in Hebrew. In the story of Moses in Genesis and elsewhere in the King James Version the Nile is referred to simply as "the river." Some authorities conjure that Gihon. One of the "four heads" of the "river that went our from Eden to water the garden," was the Nile, for Genesis 2:13 says, "The name of the second river is Gihon; it is the one which goes around the whole land of Cush."

Why was the woman taken in adultery brought to Jesus?

The story of the woman taken in adultery and brought before Jesus is one of the most widely cited passages in the entire Bible. In many respects it is one of the most beautiful and remarkable stories in the New Testament. It is found only in the Gospel of John and is not so much as alluded to in the three Synoptic Gospels (Matthew, Mark and Luke.) The incident occurred while Jesus sat in the temple and taught the people early in the morning.

John 8:3-11 says, "Then the scribes and Pharisees brought to Him a woman caught in adultery. And when they had set her in the midst, they said to Him, 'Teacher, this woman was caught in adultery, in the very act. Now Moses, in the law, commanded us that such should be stoned. But what do You say?' This they said, testing Him, that they might have something of which to accuse Him. But Jesus stooped down and wrote on the ground with His finger, as though He did not hear. So when they continued asking Him, He raised Himself up and said to them, 'He who is without sin among you, let him throw a stone at her first.' And again He stooped down and wrote on the ground. Then those who heard it, being convicted by their conscience, went out one by one, beginning with the oldest even to the last. And Jesus was left alone, and the woman standing in the midst. When Jesus had raised Himself up and saw no one but the woman, He said to her, 'Woman, where are those accusers of yours? Has no one condemned you?' She said, 'No one, Lord.' And Jesus said to her, 'Neither do I condemn you; go and sin no more.'"

The authenticity of this incident has been attacked with more vigor than almost any other part of the Bible. Higher critics are almost unanimous in saying that this passage was not part of John's original Gospel (some believe that it was originally a part of Luke); that it is not in the style of the author and the rest of John; that it breaks the normal sequence of the discourse of Jesus at that point; and that it contains several discrepancies and improbabilities. For these reasons you will find the passage printed within brackets or in a footnote in the Revised Standard Version of the Bible.

Higher critics insist that strangulation, not stoning was the historic Hebrew method of executing adulterers; that the death penalty for adultery was obsolete in the time of Jesus; that it was not a legal function of the scribes and Pharisees to accuse and bring to judgment a woman guilty of adultery, but that of the husband and the proper judges; that such a case would not be brought before Jesus for a decision, and that it is inconsistent with the rest of the Gospels for Jesus to have undertaken to judge a civil case of this kind.

Those of us who insist upon the authenticity of the passage say that it dates back to Apostolic times, even if it was not a part of some early copies of John; that the woman take in adultery may have been only betrothed, not actually married; that the sin of a betrothed woman was equivalent to a species of adultery according to rabbinic interpretation; that the enemies of Jesus wished to make Him unpopular with the people by inducing Him to revive and obsolete law; that they sought to embroil Jesus with the Romans who would not permit death penalties without their approval, and that they expected only an opinion and not a legal decision.

What is the unpardonable sin?

The words unpardonable sin do not occur in the Bible. It is the name given to the sin against the Holy Ghost or Holy Spirit because Jesus referred to it as the one sin of no forgiveness. In Matthew 12:31-32 Jesus says: "Wherefore I say unto you, All manner of sin and blasphemy shall be forgiven unto men: but the blasphemy against the Holy Ghost shall not be forgiven unto men. And whosoever speaketh a word against the Son of man, it shall be forgiven him: but whosoever speaketh against the Holy Ghost, it shall not be forgiven him, neither in this world, neither in the world to come." Similar passages occur in Mark (3:28-30) and in Luke (12:10).

Theologians differ as to the exact nature of the unpardonable sin and the subject has been difficult to penetrate. The context of the passages referred to indicates that the sin against the Holy Spirit consists of assigning His works to Satan or of denying out of pure malice the divine character of such works. When Jesus made the statement quoted above the Pharisees had accused Him of casting out devils by the prince of devils instead of by the Spirit of God.

Some commentators interpret the words "blasphemy against the Holy Ghost" in their most literal sense and define the unpardonable sin as the utterance of an insult against the Holy Spirit. Others hold the sin against the Holy Spirit to mean final impenitence of perseverance in mortal sin until death. A less rigid interpretation is that it includes all sins committed in downright malice, especially those directly opposed to charity and goodness, the characteristics of the Holy Spirit.

I John 5:16b says, "There is a sin unto death: I do not say that he shall pray for it," and while this may refer to the unpardonable sin, it more likely refers to a stubborn refusal to accept the gospel. Others imply that Hebrews 6:4-6 refers to the experience that a person must go through to commit that sin; that is to become enlightened and partake of the Holy Spirit and then fall way, but such a reading conflicts with explicit passages which teach that those whom God has truly saved will persevere in faith to the end (John 10:28, 29 and Romans 8:28-30).

The idea of an unpardonable sin comes from the Old Testament. Numbers 15:30-31 says, "But the soul that doeth ought presumptuously, whether he be born in the land, or a stranger, the same reproacheth the LORD; and that soul shall be cut off from among his people. Because he hath despised the word of the LORD, and hath broken his commandment, that soul shall utterly be cut off; his iniquity shall be upon him." That is, no sacrificial atonement was acceptable for a willful offense and under Mosaic Law a person who sinned deliberately was not forgiven. In both the Old and the New Testaments, blasphemy is the unpardonable sin. The great transgression mentioned in Psalm 19:13, "Keep back thy servant also from presumptuous sins; let them not have dominion over me: then shall I be upright, and I shall be innocent from the great transgression," refers to the same offense of presuming upon God's mercy and knowingly doing what is wrong. Such is held to be sin in the first degree.

Why did Pontius Pilate ask, "What is truth?"

The biblical passage in which Pontius Pilate, the Roman procurator of Judaea at the time Jesus was crucified, is found only in John 18:37-38. "Pilate therefore said to Him, 'Are You a king then?' Jesus answered, 'You say rightly that I am a king. For this cause I was born, and for this cause I have come into the world, that I should bear witness to the truth.

Everyone who is of the truth hears My voice.' Pilate said to Him, 'What is truth?' And when he had said this, he went out again to the Jews, and said to them, 'I find no fault in Him at all'"

This passage is generally explained on the theory that Pilate, like many Romans of his day, had come to scoff at all mention of the search for truth because the Empire was infested with all sorts of Greek sophists and Oriental theosophists who claimed to have a monopoly on truth. Pilate's question was probably rhetorical and no answer was expected.

The Gospels are remarkably lenient in their portrayal of the character of Pilate. Philo, Josephus and other ancient historians of the same period portray the Roman procurator as stubborn, cruel, vindictive and tyrannical, but the authors of the Gospels treat him with dignity and forbearance.

What happened to Pilate is the subject of several legends. He served as procurator of Judaea from about 26 A.D. until about 36 A.D., about six years after the crucifixion of Jesus. In the latter year he was summoned to Rome to answer official charges, but the Emperor Tiberius Caesar died before Pilate reached Rome. That is the last authentic information we have about him. On the basis of later legends that Pilate became a Christian, he was canonized as a saint by the Abyssinian church and is numbered among the martyrs by the Coptic Church.

There has been much concern in churches today about the appropriate form of worship. What is true worship? How do we know whether what we are doing in either in traditional worship services or in contemporary (praise) worship services is pleasing to God?

Part of the answer comes from the root meaning of the word worship. In the days during the formation of modern English (before Shakespeare) we would not have used the word worship, but instead have used the term worth-ship.

Thus, we are worshipping God when we assign Him His true worth and "glorify" His name.

Now, to glorify in early Homeric Greek meant to render an opinion. By New Testament time this Greek verb was used only for rendering a good opinion about someone and thus came to mean praise or honor. For a person to have a good opinion about God, one must be able to render a correct opinion about God's inseparable attributes (character) as revealed in Scripture. God is inseparably sovereign, omnipotent, holy, omniscient, just, omnipresent, faithful, loving, immutable, etc. God is thus worshipped, or is assigned His true worth, or is glorified when His attributes are so acknowledged.

But this is not all that is involved in worship, for God is not pleased with all worship. Jesus taught that true worship must be of the heart and not a ceremony only. "This people honors Me with their lips, but their heart is far from me; and in vain do they worship Me, teaching as doctrines the commandments of men." (Mark 7:6-7).

Throughout the Bible, God tells us more about unacceptable worship than He does about pleasing worship; several biblical references are quoted at the end of this column. Jesus tells us that true worship **must** be in "spirit and truth." (John 4:24) This does not mean being in the right place and doing certain things. Many people think they have worshipped if they have been in the right church doing the right things and at the right time. These are customs and are not worship. They may be a vehicle for real worship, but too often they become a hindrance. Worship is neither the particular things we do, nor the way in which we do them.

Worship is also not a feeling. Emotions may be stirred in real worship, but this is not worship. Neither is evangelism nor alter calls, as important as they are, worship. True worship is the adoration of God and not evangelism. True worship should cause us to evangelize, but true worship in itself is not evangelism.

Does this mean that a non-believer may be uncomfortable at true worship?

Yes, definitely, for a non-believer would find true worship completely offensive to his depraved and fallen nature. R. C. Sproul states that true worship is not "seeker sensitive." True worship is for the believer, not for the unbeliever.

True worship occurs only when our spirits, which are akin (that is related, but **not** a part of – as in pantheism or in New Age theology) to God's spirit, meet with God and praise His inseparable attributes. William Barclay wrote in his book, The Gospel of John, "True worship is when…the immortal and invisible part of man, speaks to and meets with God, who is immortal and invisible."

What bearing does all this have on the liturgy we use in our traditional or in our contemporary service? What bearing does this have on the liturgies found in other churches?

With the exception of liturgical elements that suggest wrong doctrine, no liturgy or form of worship (traditional or contemporary) is better or worse than another. Kneeling in a traditional service or hand clapping in a contemporary service is not true worship only when these activities draw our focus away from God and on the activities themselves. If we are focused on whether we are involved in a traditional or contemporary service, I would posit that we are not involved in true worship.

God-centered worship is to honor and glorify God. The purpose of each part of the worship service is to help us focus on God Himself, and not primarily how we feel. This is not to say that our response is NOT unimportant as we are to "glorify God and enjoy Him forever." However, praising and honoring God are primary. How the service affects us is secondary. The biblical pattern of worship demonstrates

God speaking to us through Scripture and our responding (by His grace) in praise, confession and thanksgiving.

If one is counting steps, one is not dancing, but only learning to dance. If one sees only letters, or words, or print, one is not reading. If one is focused of the type of church service going on, one is not worshipping. Our chief goal in worship is to focus on the true God revealed in the Bible in all of His splendor, majesty and beauty. A perfect worship service is one in which we are almost unaware of the type of service going on, as our attention is on God.

Does "Reverend" occur in the Bible?

The word "reverend" occurs in the King James Version of the Bible only once and then it refers to God. Psalm 111:9 says, "He sent redemption unto his people: he hath commanded his covenant for ever: holy and reverend is his name."

Reverend is form the same Latin root as *revere* and signifies when applied to persons, "worthy of deep respect or reverence because of age, ability, character, piety, learning, or rank." It was so used in England at the time when the King James Version was translated and was not then a title.

The title "Reverend" appears to have been first applied to the English clergy as a respectful epithet during the fifteenth century. The form, "The Reverend Mr. Robert Wilson, minister of Tamworth," was employed in 1727 and has been in general use ever since. Before reverend became a specific title, clergymen in England were customarily addressed as "Master" or "Sir."

Has glamorized Christianity with its feel-good gospel impoverished Christian worship?

Feel good worship styles tend to replace doctrinal focus, which in turn results in a decline in how we affirm our Christianity. Today most churchgoers are less willing to understand and appreciate the historical and theological context that makes Christianity what it is. Along with this comes a reduced involvement in doctrinal affairs.

Emotive worship styles have all too often supplanted doctrinal understanding. Feel good Christianity has tended to replace the nuts and bolts of our creeds and confessions. It is a shift that ill serves our churches for it diverts our attention from substantive biblical, theological and doctrinal concerns and offers bogus solutions that often re-design God into a genie.

When emotions are not balanced with intellect we end up focusing on <u>our</u> concept of God, rather than God as He has revealed Himself in Scripture. According to Dr. R. C. Sproul, the heart (hence our emotions) follows the mind; our mind does not follow our heart. The author of Romans clearly states that we are transformed by the renewing of our mind, not our heart. In Romans 12:2 we read, "And do not be conformed to this world, but be transformed by the renewing of your mind, that you may prove what is that good and acceptable and perfect will of God."

The purpose of worship is for believers to focus on God and to worship Him in spirit and in truth. The purpose of worship is not to build an audience, but to build the Church, the Bride of Christ. The "casual" direction that many church services are taking belies the basic principle of giving the Lord our very best. Paul Harvey commented that people would dress up to meet the queen of England and other dignitaries, but yet believe they can dress down to meet the King of Kings. A "come as you are" mentality is demeaning to the place where God's honor resides.

In our worship we must exalt Christ over culture, restrain market forces, and stick with biblically based doctrine. When marketing to "seekers" becomes the emphasis, churches become focused on programs, and that is idolatry.

Bible based, theologically sound worship services are not boring. Worship in the early church was so boisterous than many people thought the Christians were drunk. Paul's sermons were so riveting that the crowds listened until midnight. Christianity is not a product to be marketed to the gullible. The preaching of the "Old Rugged Cross" is not the merchandise of a feel-good product. Gourmet coffee and doughnuts, contemporary "bait and switch" sales tactics, and carnival like atmospheres do not satisfy our longing to know Jesus Christ, both as Lord and as Savior.

If the "Big Bang" theorists were proven to be right, wouldn't that disprove the biblical story of creation?

Not in the least. There probably was a "big bang" when God created the heavens and the earth *ex nihilo*, that is, out of nothing. God's creative activity was not an ordering of preexisting matter.

It is quite logical to say that God is self-existing. Theologians speak of this as God's *aseity*, (from the Latin *a se*, which means "from Himself"). Theologians also speak of God as *sui generis*, in a class by Himself. However, it requires a great leap of logic to speak matter and energy as self-existing and in a class by themselves. Thus, the "Big Bang" theorists need to explain the "Uncaused Cause" that created the stuff (matter and energy) of the Big Bang. They also have to deal with the notion that the laws that govern creation are not merely statistically improbable, but that these laws are so irreducibly complex that the heavens themselves proclaim the glory of the Lord!

Will we be reunited with our loved ones in heaven?

Resurrection is the hope of Christianity. Jesus said, "In My Father's house are many mansions; if it were not so, I would have told you. I go to prepare a place for you. And if I go and prepare a place for you, I will come again and receive you to Myself; that where I am, there you may be also" (John 14:2-3).

Jesus promises that all who come to believe in Him will have eternal life and will be lifted up at the last day (John 6:40). Moreover, Jesus informs us that not one of us can (that is, is able to) come to believe in Him unless the Father draws (literally as one draws water from a well) us. "No one can come to Me unless the Father who sent Me draws him; and I will raise him up at the last day" (John 6:44). And then in John 6:47, Jesus reiterates, "Most assuredly, I say to you, he who believes in Me has everlasting life." Therefore, we may conclude that those who have come to believe on Jesus will be in heaven together.

In the Old Testament, we see this hope clearly stated in David's experience, after he lost his firstborn child with Bethsheba. "And he (David) said, 'While the child was alive, I fasted and wept; for I said, 'Who can tell whether the Lord will be gracious to me, that the child may live?' But now he is dead; why should I fast? Can I bring him back again? <u>I shall go to him</u> (underlining mine), but he shall not return to me'" (Second Samuel 12:22-23)

The last book the New Testament, the book of Revelation, testifies that salvation awaits all who are redeemed by the blood of Christ. "And they sang a new song, saying: 'You are worthy to take the scroll, And to open its seals; For You were slain, And have redeemed us to God by Your blood Out of every tribe and tongue and people and nation'" (Revelation 5:9).

It is this hope of a heavenly reunion with our family and friends in a place beyond our wildest dreams that compels those of us drawn by the Father to share our faith.

Since my spouse was married before, who will be the mate of my spouse in heaven?

The Sadducees posed a similar question to Jesus in Luke 20:27-33. This is the only place in which Luke mentions the Sadducees who were conservative and aristocratic. They rejected the tradition of the Pharisees and did not believe in the doctrine of the resurrection in the Old Testament.

In an attempt to make nonsense of the resurrection, the Sadducees spoke of a woman who married into a family of seven brothers. Upon the death of her husband, this childless widow marries his brother, who also dies. She then marries the third brother, who likewise dies. The saga continues until she has married all seven.

The question the Sadducees raise is similar to yours. They ask whose wife will she be in the resurrection. The Sadducees, like you, erroneously assumed that if there were an afterlife it would be the same as this life.

While marriage is an essential part of this life, it is not an essential part of our heavenly life. Jesus answered the Sadducees in John 20:34-35, "The sons of this age (this life, or this world) marry and are given in marriage. But those who are counted worthy to attain that age (the life to come, or heaven), and the resurrection from the dead, neither marry nor are given in marriage." Therefore, spousal relationships (marriage) and procreation will not be necessary or appropriate to our immortal heavenly bodies.

Isn't reincarnation possible?

Statistically, reincarnation or the transmigration of souls (metempsychosis) is "possible" but highly improbable. Biblically, reincarnation is impossible.

The purpose of reincarnation is for the progressive purification or evolutionary development of the soul. It is widely believed in Eastern religions like Buddhism and Hinduism. It was also taught in the Greek traditions of Pythagoreanism, Platonism, and by the Neoplatonists of the Italian Renaissance. Today one finds advocates of reincarnation among astrologists, New Age religionists like Shirley MacLaine, spiritualists and theosophists like Emanual Swedenborg.

Reincarnation lacks biblical support. The bible clearly teaches that, "And as it is appointed for men to die once but after this the judgment" (Hebrews 9:27).

Moreover, reincarnation carries with it a notion of justification by works, that one has to earn one's reward to a higher level in one's next incarnation. Any system of justification by works is antithetical with Scripture.

The Bible clearly states that a man is, "not justified by the works of the law but by faith in Jesus Christ, even we have believed in Christ Jesus, that we might be justified by faith in Christ and not by the works of the law; for by the works of the law no flesh shall be justified" (Galatians 2:16). "For by grace you have been saved through faith, and that not of yourselves; it is the gift of God, not of works, lest anyone should boast" (Ephesians 2:8-9).

In the truly postmodern world, who is to say who is right and who is wrong or what is truth? Are there not many correct or right answers to most questions?

Indeed in the postmodern world, what counts as truth is how you feel about it and what you do with it. "Truth" has become subjective, multiple and relative.

As a result, in the postmodern world, religion is in, but truth is out. It seems that many have discovered, in an almost giddy happiness, that religion once again is the in thing. Books on angels sell like latté at the Walden and even Christian bookstores. It does not seem to matter that the angels about whom most people talk are virtually indistinguishable from the gods and goddesses of our theological ancestors in Europe, Africa and Asia.

In the postmodern world there are many "correct or right answers" to most questions, regardless of the context. What postmodernists concentrate on is feeling and relating, for that alone makes their postmodern world worth living. Few people ask anymore, "What do you believe about this?

Or what do you think about this?" Instead the question is, "How do you feel about this?" In the past what was true or untrue had been based on fact, on what is, and by communities; but in postmodernism, each individual, based mainly on how one "feels about it," defines truth. Instead of churches reforming in accordance with the Word of God, churches have been conforming to the values of secular culture, and thus are deforming by modern, relativistic thinking.

Truth based on fact has been replaced by the tyranny of individual preferences. Those considered heretics in our postmodern age are: (1) those who insist that there is a truth of God's law (a natural law) that underlies all of creation; and (2) those of us who hold to our duty as creatures of our God, and as servants of our Savior to discern that truth, and then in the light of that truth, reform both our personal lives and the very structure of the world of human knowledge and experience.

In Christianity truth does not come initially through the power of human reason, because reason can never enlighten on its own. Instead truth arises out of the insight provided by "revelation," which in turn, may be, and often is, substantiated by reason. For Christianity, truth is objective, singular and absolute.

This dichotomy of worldviews was recently evidenced when Auburn University History Professor J. Wayne Flynt said of Alabama Supreme Court Chief Justice Ray Moore's stand on posting the Ten Commandments monument in the state judicial building, that Moore "lives in a world where there isn't any gray — which makes him really scary."

In the Christian world there is only one correct or right answer within the context of any question. Furthermore, the correct or right answer arises out of the illumination of God's Word revealed in the sacred Scriptures and pointing to Jesus Christ without whom nothing in this universe had been created (John 1:3) and in whom all things finally hold together (Colossians 1:17). Christianity does not separate faith from knowledge. We believe so that we might know. It is only out of faith that we gain knowledge of the truth that flows from the One whom we know in faith.

The challenge then for Christians (in this postmodern world that increasingly dismisses the possibility of a single, objective, and absolute truth; a world where even scholars place the word "truth" in quotation marks as if to question its validity; a world where "feeling" and personal choice reign supreme over God's Word of creation and revelation) is to stand fast for the One who is the Truth.

What is Open Theism?

The tenets of open theism deny God's exhaustive knowledge of the future. While this theological movement affirms some aspects of the classical view of God, such as, God's independence, the Trinity, creation, and relational capability, it rejects some of the classical views of God's attributes, specifically the changelessness of God and the divine foreknowledge of human choices.

The name "open theism" derives from the affirmation that God Himself is open to new experiences, including the experience of learning the progressive events of world history as the events unfold. It emphasizes God's self-limitation in dealing with human beings. Because God desires people's free response, openness theologians say, God neither predetermines nor foreknows their moral choices. In the Bible they say God changes His mind, or "repents," in response to human actions.

The leaders of open theism are articulate, well-educated, evangelicals affirming the inerrancy of Scripture. The "great triumvirate" of open theism includes Clark Pinnock, Gregory Boyd and John Sanders. Pinnock, recently retired professor of theology at McMaster Divinity College in Ontario, Canada, is a British scholar who began his North American teaching career at New Orleans Baptist Theological Seminary in the 1960s. Gregory Boyd formerly taught at Bethel College, associated with the Baptist General Conference, in St. Paul, Minnesota. John Sanders teaches at Huntington College in Huntington, Indiana, a Brethren in Christ school.

Throughout Christian history, orthodox believers expressed a common understanding of the nature of God labeled "classical theism." Classical theism affirms that God is unchanging in His being, character, purposes and promises. Thomas Oden, professor of theology at Drew University, strongly disagrees with the openness position. In a Feb. 9, 1998, *Christianity Today* article, Oden wrote, "The fantasy that God is ignorant of the future is a heresy that must be rejected on scriptural grounds."

In 2002, the Evangelical Theological Society (ETS) passed a simple resolution affirming God's foreknowledge by a vote of 253 to 66 with 66 members abstaining. The resolution stated, "We believe the Bible clearly teaches that God has complete, accurate, and infallible knowledge of all events past, present, and future, including all future decisions and actions of free moral agents."

The presenters at a "Walk to Emmaus" weekend frequently spoke of "prevenient grace." What is prevenient grace?

Simply stated, prevenient grace is God's enabling or preparing work in the heart of the sinner, turning the sinner toward faith in the redemptive work of Christ. Since it is grace, it is a free gift from God that cannot be earned or merited in anyway.

Early in church history, a theologian by the name of Pelagius vehemently disagreed with Augustine. Pelagius denied that God must grant by grace the ability to humans to do what God commands. According to Pelagius self-acquired virtue is the supreme good. Our own righteousness may be won at any moment by our own efforts. Pelagius was condemned as a heretic at the Synod of Carthage (418) and at the Council of Ephesus (431) settling the controversy over the need for grace for salvation.

The question surrounding prevenient grace is whether it is operative or cooperative. When we speak of operative prevenient grace we mean that God moves the human will to will the good, or to believe. Cooperative prevenient grace means that God moves the human will to will the good and the human will wills the good, or believes on its own following initial assistance from God. Like my namesake Augustine (with whom Aquinas, Luther and Calvin concurred), I would also say prevenient grace is operative rather than cooperative since faith is exercised by the believer and not the unregenerate.

God alone performs the work of regeneration. This grace of regeneration precedes faith. We are "born again" or "born from above" first, and then we believe. We do not believe and then become born again for then our redemption would be of our own efforts. Paul tells us in Ephesians 2:8, "For by grace you have been saved through faith, and that not of yourselves; it is the gift of God." Any cooperation on our part occurs only after God's operative gift of regeneration has been accomplished.

Who said, "be sure your sin will find you out?"

This saying, which has become proverbial, is attributed to Moses. Moses agreed to permit the children of Reuben and Gad and the half-tribe of Manasseh to settle permanently east of the Jordan provided their fighting men would help the other tribes conquer and claim the Promised Land. In Numbers 32:23, Moses says to them, "But if you do not do so, then take note, you have sinned against the Lord; and be sure your sin will find you out."

How did "holier than thou" originate?

"Holier than thou," which is applied to persons who profess to be more virtuous than other people, is taken from the Old Testament. According to Isaiah 65:5, the Israelites, who reveled against Jehovah and went after their own thoughts, said, "Keep to yourself, Do not come near me, For I am holier than thou."

Jesus gives a good example of the holier than thou type in the parable of the Pharisee and the publican who went up into the temple to pray. In his prayer the self-righteous Pharisee bragged of his compliance with the technical requirements of his religion and thanked God that he was not like other men.

Does the Bible say human beings were once vegetarians?

It appears from passages in Genesis that mankind did not eat the flesh of animals before the flood. According to Genesis 1:29 God said to Adam and Eve: "See, I have given you every herb that yields seed which is on the face of all the earth, and every tree whose fruit yields seed; to you it shall be for food."

But after the flood permission to eat animals as food was granted. In Genesis 9:3, God said to Noah and his sons, "Every moving thing that lives shall be food for you. I have given you all things, even as the green herbs." The term "every moving thing" obviously includes all animal life — beast, fish, and fowl. This passage seems to signify that just as the green herb was granted to mankind for food at the beginning, later we were given permission to eat the flesh of animal life.

Is the desire for sex wrong?

In what we call the Sermon on the Mount, our Lord Jesus Christ deals with the sanctity of sexual relations. His teaching on this is introduce in Matthew 5:27, "You have heard that it was said to those of old, 'You shall not commit adultery.'" In the very next verse, He adds, "But I say to you that whoever looks at a woman to lust for her has already committed adultery with her in his heart," which statement contrasts with the teaching of the scribes and Pharisees, who had confined adultery to the overt act only. Jesus teaching included reference to the lascivious desire of the heart as well as the outward act. The pivot of Jesus' indirect clause is "to lust for her." It is the "lustful" desire upon which Jesus places His finger of reproof.

However, Jesus does not say that all sexual desire is wrong. To cast any aspersion on sex desire is to impugn the integrity of our Creator God and His creation. It is not wrong to satisfy our sexual desire and impulse in the way God has ordained. Scripture fully recognizes the propriety of that motive and commends marriage as the honorable and necessary outlet for our sexual impulse. What is wrong is to satisfy the impulse to the sex act outside of marriage.

Premarital sex is very widespread today and is almost taken for granted. The language used in the media and in educational circles makes its own value judgments: teens are no longer "promiscuous" (much less engaging in "fornication"), but rather have chosen to become "sexually active." Such language is neither neutral nor objective, but implies the legitimacy of sex outside of marriage. "Active" is such a strong and positive word that the "sexually inactive" must be unhealthy or abnormal or "hung-up," or so it would seem.

The biblical teaching on the illicitness of sexual intercourse outside of marriage is clear and unequivocal. Fornication is defined in the Theological Dictionary of the New Testament as an "unconditional repudiation of all extramarital and unnatural intercourse." The Interpreter's Bible Dictionary concurs and defines fornication or the practice of fornication as "every kind of sexual intercourse outside of marriage."

These conclusions are easily confirmed by an inspection of representative New Testament texts. No fornicator has any part in the Kingdom of God, I Corinthians 6:9, although repentance and forgiveness mean a new start, I Corinthians 6:11. Fornication and sexual uncleanness are repeatedly mentioned in the lists of vices the Christian is to avoid (Romans 1:24-32; I Corinthians 5:10f., 6:9f.; II Corinthians 12:20f.; Galatians 5:19-21; Colossians 3:5, 8f.). Toleration of the fornicator endangers the spiritual well being of the church (I Corinthians 5:1f.). God's will for the believer is sanctification and sexual purity (I Thessalonians 4:1-5). Problems of sexual immorality are rebuked in the church of Pergamum (Revelation 2:14) and at Thyatira (Revelation 2:20). The author of Revelation warns that the persistent and unrepentant fornicator is in danger of the second death (Revelation 21:8, 22:15).

The disturbing trends in American public health confirm the Bible's teaching that those who sow to the flesh will from the flesh reap corruption (Galatians 6:8). Persistent violation by any society of the basic principal of natural moral law will eventually reap its consequences. The British anthropologist J. D. Unwin, on the basis of a comprehensive study of ancient and modern civilizations, concluded that, "the whole of human history does not contain a single instance of a group becoming civilized unless it has become absolutely monogamous, nor is there any example of a group retaining its culture after it has adopted less rigorous customs" (*Monogamy as a Condition of Social Energy*, The Hibbert Journal 25, pp. 663-677.). In the long run we don't break God's laws; they break us.

As New Testament believers aren't we under grace and not law?

The New Testament believer is not without law to God but under law to Christ. The New Testament believer delights in the law of God after the inward man and therefore reiterates the exclamation of the Old Testament saint, "Oh, how I love Your law! It is my meditation all the day" (Psalm 119:97).

Also, the New Testament believer is not forgetful that He (Jesus Christ), who was the incarnation and embodiment of virtue, who is the supreme and perfect example, said, "I delight to do Your will, O my God, And Your law is within my heart" (Psalm 40:8, Matthew 26:39; John 4:34, 6:38; Hebrews 10:7).

What is the most often quoted verse in the Bible?

Until 30 or 40 years ago the answer would have been, John 3:16, "For God so loved the world that He gave His only begotten Son, that whoever believes in Him should not perish but have everlasting life." Today, as many pastors, theologians and Christian researchers point out, the most frequently quoted passage from Scripture is Matthew 7:1, "Judge not, that you be not judged."

We live in a society where, for most, truth is no longer absolute, but is considered relative; where truth is no longer singular, but is viewed as multiple; where truth is no longer objective, but is subjective. In much of today's society it is ok to "do our own thing" and who is to judge that our behavior is inappropriate. We no longer abide by an absolute standard of ethical behavior given to us from on high, but instead we abide by our own evolving normative moral standards. We have erroneously attempted to make "what is" into what "should be."

Since society's new view on "truth" is antithetical with what Scripture defines as Truth, society has taken false comfort in the words of Jesus found in Matthew 7:1. When believers try to address abhorrent behavior, society confronts with "Judge not, that you be not judged." We believers need to note that this quote from the first verse in Matthew chapter seven, is taken out of context.

The entire seventh chapter actually commands us to judge. While Jesus is prohibiting one kind of judging, He goes on to approve a different kind. What Jesus is saying is that it is wrong to only condemn others for their faults, but that we must instead render humble and gentle criticism that first recognizes our own faults. Jesus goes on to approve of a discerning kind of judgment that does not condemn but distinguishes unbelief from belief, unholy from holy, evil from good, wide and narrow gates, wolves from sheep, etc. all of which cannot be done without judging.

When is Reformation Day and what is its significance?

October 31 is Reformation Day. Dr. D. James Kennedy has noted that many Protestants have no more idea of what the Reformation was about than they could explain to you the special Theory of Relativity. They are members of a church by accident of birth, and they attend by mere habit. Many would have no more idea when they went into a church whether the preacher was preaching the Gospel or whether he was preaching the absolute antithesis to it.

October 31, 1517 was the day in which an Augustinian monk, Martin Luther nailed his 95 thesis to the church door in Whittenberg as an invitation to scholars in the church to debate those issues. What Martin Luther did 486 years ago, was to shatter centuries of dogma and tradition that had hidden the Gospel from the world. Up until that time, the Gospel of grace had been overlaid with hundreds of years of accretion of human merit. Everywhere men and women, by their own strivings and their own pious endeavors, sought to save themselves by good works.

The major debate back in the 16th. Century centered not on the sale of indulgences, the role of the papacy, penance, purgatory or Mary and saints, but on the article of how is a person justified. These other items on which Roman Catholics and Protestants differ, all hinge on our respective view of justification and the role of works in our justification. To this day, this article of how one is justified continues as the focal point or the difference between our theologies. This difference may be expressed in two formulas:

> Roman Catholic theology says: Faith (by grace) + Works ⇒ Justification
> Protestant theology replies: Faith (by grace) ⇒ Justification + Works

All other differences between Roman Catholicism and Protestantism are mere trifles. What is at stake here is the Gospel itself. It answers the question raised by the Philippian jailer to Paul, "What must I do to be saved?" We are not engaged in a controversy over whether to sprinkle, dip or immerse but of salvation itself. It is the most important question we have as Christians. It is the problem of the justice of God. God is just and you and I are not. David raised that question is antiquity when he asked, "If the Lord mark iniquities, who would stand?"

If God is not going to negotiate His justice, how are we saved? This was the debate of the 16th. century between Luther and Rome and which continues today between Roman Catholicism and evangelical Protestantism. Does God wait until we become just before He declares us just, or does He declare us just in His site before we are just? Luther's formula was *simul iustus et pecator*, translated as at the same time just and sinner. That is we are justified by the work of Christ yet we still sin.

Rome heard in this formula a legal fiction. It would be unworthy, they say, of God and make Him a liar to declare a person just before a person is indeed just. Roman Catholicism agrees that justification occurs when God declares one to be just, but He does not do so, according to Rome, until one is indeed just.

The Reformers countered that it is not a legal fiction, but a legal diction. It is a legal diction by the One who does the justifying. God declares one just on the basis of the real work (the life and the death) of Christ. One is justified by faith, and that little word by, is the means through which one is justified as Christ both lived and died for us.

Roman Catholicism has two instrumental causes of justification, baptism and penance. Protestantism has only one, faith that lays hold of the merit of Christ. The critical questions then are: Is justification infused through the Roman sacraments of baptism and penance? Or is justification imputed (transferred) to us by the righteousness of Christ? A righteousness that is not in the believer, but a righteousness that is for the believer. Is it justification by infusion or by imputation?

Reformation or Protestant theology holds to the latter. Justification for Protestants means to have the perfect righteous of Jesus Christ clothe them as a white robe, as their sins were ALL imputed to Christ at Calvary. Christ's righteous life is also imputed to them who are thus made faultless to stand before the eyes of an all-holy God. Salvation for Protestants is by grace alone through Christ alone. It is unearned, undeserved and unmerited. It is received by a simple trust in Christ.

How do we answer secular humanists who question why didn't an all-good and powerful God just forgive us instead of going through the process of slaughtering His own Child?

Saint Anselm in his great work, Cur Deus Homo? written at the end of the eleventh century, wrote, "If anybody imagines that God can simply forgive us as we forgive others, that person has not yet considered the seriousness of sin. That person has not yet considered the majesty of God. It is when our perception of God and man, or of holiness and sin, are askew that our understanding of the atonement is bound to be askew also?

"The crucial question we should ask, is not why God finds it difficult to forgive, but how He finds it possible to do so at all. Forgiveness is to man the plainest of duties; to God it is the profoundest of problems. The problem of forgiveness is constituted by the inevitable collision between divine perfection and human rebellion, between God as He is and us as we are. On the cross divine mercy and justice were equally expressed and eternally reconciled. God's holy love was satisfied."

That knowledge, that certainty, of which Anselm wrote, has caused millions of Christians to be willing to die a martyr's death, even to this very century, is what infuriates the unbelieving world of the secular humanist. That is what the unbeliever cannot understand. Like Pilate they cynically sneer, "What is truth? No man can know the truth."

To which sneer comes the reply of Jesus eternally, "I am the way, the truth and the life. No man comes to the Father but by me. I am the good shepherd; and I know My sheep, and am known by My own. As the Father knows Me, even so I know the Father; and I lay down My life for the sheep. And you shall know the truth, and the truth shall make you free."

How can I know if I am one of God's chosen people?

The Bible clearly tells us that if you have faith in God you are one of God's chosen people. We do not work out such faith for ourselves, but rather such faith comes to us purely as a gift from God. Ephesians 2:8-9 states, "For by grace you have been saved through faith, and that (*that is that faith is*) not of yourselves; it is the gift of God, not of works, lest anyone should boast." First John 5:13 assures us that, "These things I have written to you who believe in the name of the Son of God, that you may *know* that you have eternal life."

However, being chosen has its burdens as well as its blessings. Tevye, the beloved dairyman in "Fiddler on the Roof" observed, when he dryly suggested that maybe, "for once (God could) choose someone else." From Tevye's perspective, being the chosen people had a high price (persecutions, wanderings and broken dreams) while the benefit package remained illusive and ill defined.

Some have struggled with the concept of the Jews being God's chosen people and question what makes the Jews think they are so special that God would choose them over all other people? Such questions thinly disguise the resentment that has often boiled up into vehement anti-Semitism. That resentment provoked one to write, "How odd of God to choose the Jews, but not so odd as those who choose the Jewish God and hate the Jews." The oddness stems from a failure to realize that chosen-ness reflects more on the One who chooses than on those who are chosen. God's choosing is meant to raise our awareness of His character, rather than to raise the status of those He has chosen. In choosing the Jewish people, God demonstrated to us and to the entire world that he is a loving God who is faithful to keep all His promises.

Nevertheless, the Jewish people are not God's only chosen ones. The Hebrew word for chosen is *bachar*, and the church of Jesus Christ is the chosen of God. "For this reason

I endure all things for the sake of those who are chosen, so that they also may obtain the salvation which is in Christ Jesus (and) with (it) eternal glory." (Second Timothy 2:10)

When God chooses people, He asks us to be different from the rest of the world. The rest of the world has a problem with that. When we don't do as they do, they feel judged and they view us as the source of it. Of course God is the Judge. He sets the standards. He determined the basis upon which the descendants of Abraham, Isaac, and Jacob would be called out as the chosen people. Likewise, God has determined the basis on which people can enter a relationship with Him today. That is the basis of the new covenant and faith in Jesus Christ, a faith that sets us apart from the rest of the world.

Jesus clearly tells us in John 6:44 that we cannot come to Him (that is have faith in Him) on our own, but only if God, the Father, gives us that faith. Let's analyze what Jesus is saying here, "No one can come to Me unless the Father who sent Me draws him." "No man" is a universal negative. If Jesus said "All men" it would be a universal positive, but Jesus is clearly stating that absolutely no one can (that is no one has the ability) to come to Him. Jesus is not saying that no one "may come" to Him, which would mean that no one has permission to come to Him, but that no one is able to come to Him, "unless" a necessary condition is met. And the necessary condition is that one must be drawn (literally dragged) by the Father to Him.

There is a "theologically correct" scene in the movie "O God" where John Denver runs into a Synagogue and tells a Rabbi the he wants to "find God." The rabbi correctly informs him that, "You don't find God; God finds you!"

Likewise we don't choose God; God chooses us. When God chooses people He charges them with a responsibility as well as a relationship. Part of that responsibility is to obey the commands that make us different from the world, and part of that responsibility is to invite the world into the Kingdom of God. Let us rejoice then in the high and holy calling He has placed on us to whom He has given such faith and thus are His chosen people.

Why does the honor guard pay meticulous attention to correctly folding the American flag 13 times?

Before putting my reply in print, I confirmed my answer with a former commandant of the Air War College of Air War University, of which I am an alumn. Most think the meticulous folding of the flag is to symbolize the original 13 colonies, but as you read on you will find that is not the case.

The 1st fold of our flag is a symbol of life. The 2nd fold is a symbol of our belief in eternal life. The 3rd fold is made in honor and remembrance of the veterans departing our ranks who gave a portion of their lives for the defense of our country to attain peace throughout the world.

The 4th fold represents our weaker nature, for as American citizens trusting in God it is to Him we turn in times of peace, as well as in time of war, for His divine guidance. The 5th fold is a tribute to our country, for in the words of Stephen Decaur, "Our Country, in dealing with other countries, may she always be right; but it is still our country, right or wrong."

The 6th fold is for where our hearts lie. It is with our heart that we "pledge allegiance to the flag of the United States of America, and to the Republic for which it stands, one Nation under God, indivisible, with Liberty and Justice for all." The 7th fold is a tribute to our Armed Forces, for it is through the Armed Forces that we protect our country and our flag against all her enemies, whether they are found within or without the boundaries of our republic.

The 8th fold is a tribute to the One who entered into the valley of the shadow of death, that we might see the light of day. The 9th fold is a tribute to womanhood and mothers, for it has been through their faith, love, loyalty and devotion that the character of the men and women who have made this country great have been molded. The 10th fold is a tribute to fatherhood and fathers, for they too have given their sons and daughters for the defense of our country.

The 11th fold represents the lower portion of the seal of King David and King Solomon and glorifies the God of Abraham, Isaac and Jacob. The 12th fold represents an emblem of eternity and glorifies God - the Father, the Son and Holy Spirit. After the 13th or final fold, the stars are uppermost reminding us of our nation's motto, "In God We Trust."

After the flag is completely folded and tucked in, it takes on the appearance of a cocked hat, ever reminding us of the soldiers who served under General George Washington, and the sailors and marines who served under Captain John Paul Jones, who were followed by their comrades and shipmates in the Armed Forces of the United States, preserving for us the rights, privileges, freedoms, and responsibilities we enjoy today. Our traditions do have deep meaning. In the future, when you see flags meticulously folded, you will know why.

Is *In God We Trust* in the Bible?

In God We Trust, the motto on all United States coins, is not in the Bible, but it may have been suggested indirectly by various biblical phrases. According the Psalms 56:11, David sang, "In God I have put my trust, I shall not be afraid." In Job 13:15, the patriarch said to the Almighty, "Though He slay me, I will trust Him." According to Matthew 27:43, the chief priests, scribes and elders, mocking Jesus on the cross, said, "HE TRUSTS IN GOD: LET HIM DELIVER *HIM* now, IF HE TAKES PLEASURE IN HIM; for He said, 'I am the Son of God.'"

The underlying thought of *In God We Trust*, though not expressed in these exact words, was current long before the motto was first placed on United States coins. Francis Scott Key's *The Star Spangled Banner*, which was first printed in *The Baltimore Patriot* on September 20, 1814, under the title *Defense of Fort McHenry*, contains the couplet, "Then conquer we must, for out cause it is just, And this be our motto: 'In God is our trust'." In a letter dated April 25, 1861, and addressed to Cassius Lee, Robert E. Lee acknowledged that mediation between the Northern and Southern States was impossible and declared that, "In God must be our trust." It was during that same year that the Reverend W. R. Watkinson of Ridleyville. Pennsylvania, wrote to Secretary of Treasury Salmon P. Chase suggesting that the Deity be recognized in some form on American coins.

Acting upon this suggestion, Secretary Chase instructed James Pollock, director of the United States Mint at Philadelphia, to have prepared without delay a device with a motto expressing such national recognition of the Deity. Secretary Chase wrote, "No nation can be strong except in the strength of God or safe except in His defense. The trust of our people in God should be declared on our national coins." Owing to legal difficulties, Pollock did not submit his designs until 1863. One of the mottoes suggested was *God Our Trust*. At a cabinet meeting during that same year it was proposed to place *In God We Trust* on paper money as well as on coins.

President Lincoln, however, observed dryly that if a legend was to be engraved on the greenbacks he would suggest that of Peter in Acts 3:6. "Silver and gold have I none; but such as I have give I Thee." In 1864 Congress passed an act authorizing the coinage of the two-cent piece, and it was upon these bronze two-cent pieces that the motto *In God We Trust* first appeared. Later Congress passed an act giving the proper officials authority to place the motto on all coins that would have space for the inscription.

During the second administration of Theodore Roosevelt, Augustus St. Gaudens, the sculptor, prepared some designs for new coins with a view to improving the coinage from an artistic standpoint. When the double eagle and eagle of the new designs appeared in 1907, the motto *In God We Trust* was omitted. President Roosevelt objected to the motto on the coins on the grounds that such use of the beautiful sentiment tended to cheapen it. A storm of criticism all over the country was the result.

Once a design for a coin is approved and accepted, it cannot be changed under the law within twenty-five years without an act of Congress. Therefore an act of Congress was required to restore *In God We Trust* on the eagle and the double eagle. This was done by a bill that passed Congress in 1908, providing that, "the motto *In God We Trust* heretofore inscribed on certain denominations of gold and silver coins of the United States of America, shall hereafter be inscribed upon all such gold and silver coins of said denominations as heretofore."

What is wrong with the "para-church" feel good worship style?

Several weeks ago as I was walking around a lake in the suburban area north of Orlando, I came upon a small billboard advertising a new "para-church" that was meeting in the community. In addition to listing the name and meeting place of the church, the billboard contained these words, "Where church is NEVER normal."

As I stood and read, I could not help thinking how far the "para-church" has traded sound theological doctrine for the philosophy of pragmatism. Since when is it appropriate to speak of the Church, "bride of Christ, the body of Christ, the family of God, the elect, the redeemed, the communion of saints, the people of God" as "never normal."

Pragmatism ultimately defines truth as that which is useful, as that which works. It is inherently relativistic, rejecting the notion of absolute right and wrong. Biblical truth is not determined by testing what works and what does not. Scriptural truth holds to absolutes in what is right and wrong.

Nevertheless, an overpowering surge of ardent pragmatism is sweeping across the nation especially in these "para-churches." Why? Because these "para-churches" believe they will get more people in their buildings by amusing people, giving them success tips and pop-psychology instead of the Gospel. They emphasize experiences, how people "feel" about issues and they de-emphasize doctrine. When Biblical truth is preached, it is offered in small, diluted doses.

Idolatry has always been more popular than true worship. True worship is often being discarded or downplayed in these "para-churches" in favor drama, dance, comedy, variety, side-show histrionics, pop-psychology and other entertainment forms just to draw larger crowds. The purpose of worship is not to entertain us. We are not the audience in worship, God is. It is little wonder that this new "para-church" boasts of being more rollicking than reverent. Theology has taken a back seat to methodology.

Don't get me wrong. I recognize that styles of worship are always in flux and that even our most traditional worship services today would bear little resemblance to those of centuries ago when there was no organ, public address system, PowerPoint and men and women often worshipped separately. I am not in favor of a stagnant church nor am I bound to any particular musical or liturgical style in worship. I am opposed to interpreting the Great Commission as a marketing manifesto.

How we worship is ultimately determined by our doctrine of God. For example, the deities of primitive cultures were offered sacrifices in worship to appease their wrath.

Until the last third of the 20th. Century, worship in Evangelical Protestant and Roman Catholic churches focused on the Word and the administration of the sacraments in accordance with appropriate church dogma. (Dogma sets forth in an organized and topical form the doctrinal content of the Christian faith. Doctrine states what the Bible and the church, in accordance with the Bible, teach about a particular topic.)

Before the late 1960's most Christians held to a common doctrine of God, man, sin, Christ, the Holy Spirit, the church, etc. Denominationally, Christians differed on various doctrines concerning the sacraments and justification. They also held to common as well as distinctive creeds and confessions. Worship often included an affirmation of doctrines through the recitation of these creeds and confessions.

Over the past four decades we have experienced a decline in the formality of our worship and how we affirm our Christianity. Today, few worshipping Christians can recite the Apostles and the Nicene creeds from memory, although I am not implying that mere memorization be a test for true belief. Fewer still know what early Christian heresies caused them to be written.

Many contemporary Christians express displeasure when the Ten Commandments are removed from courtrooms and schoolrooms. Yet they remain silent when the reading of these Commandments (once a common practice) is no longer included in today's worship settings. Some further show a lack of doctrinal understanding when they defend not including the Commandments in worship because we "are under grace." Without the law, there can be no grace. God is indeed love, but He is also holy and just.

All this points to the fact that today's worshipping Christian is less willing and able to understand the historical and theological context that makes Christianity what it is. Along with this comes a reduced involvement in doctrinal affairs. Emotive worship styles have all too often supplanted doctrinal understandings.

Feel good Christianity has tended to replace the nuts and bolts of our creeds and confessions. It is a shift that ill serves our churches for it diverts our attention from substantive theological and doctrinal concerns and offers in their place, bogus solutions — solutions like adding feminine writings to Scripture, blessing same sex unions, and ordaining *practicing* homosexuals and other *non*-repentant sinners.

God must first be in our heads before He can be in our hearts. When we give way to "emotional expressivism" in worship, emotions are not balanced with intellect and the resulting worship style focuses on our concept of God, rather than on God as He is, as He has revealed Himself in Scripture and in a tradition that is in accord with that Scripture.

Although Christians should be solemnly warned not to be schismatic in spirit or given to divisive or quarrelsome spirits, they must also be warned of the obligation to separate themselves from false, apostate communions or "parachurches." The "normal" church transcends history yet remains concretely historical. Although the reformation of the church in accordance with the Word of God is a never-ending task, every true church exhibits the true marks of a church to some degree. Thus, the "normal" church seeks to be more and more faithful to (1) the true preaching of God's Word, (2) the proper administration of the sacraments, and (3) the faithful exercise of church discipline to collaborate as disciples of Christ for the sake of the Kingdom of God.

Is God's love unconditional?

Although God's love is not based upon any condition found in us, it is conditional upon what He did for us. Therefore, in this sense God's love is not unconditional.

Do you remember that hit song during the 1950's that rose into the top ten on the Hit Parade listings? The title was

"He" and the words mainly sang of God's almighty power over His creation. But do you remember the last line of that song? It stated, "He'll always say, I forgive." Is that really true? Does the Bible teach us that God will always (unconditionally) say, "I forgive?"

Although it has become fashionable to speak of God's unconditional love, where in Scripture do we find this exaggerated expression of the unconditional love of God? Isn't God's love conditional on what He did for us? If God's love were absolutely unconditional then there would be no need for the cross and for people to repent and to be reconciled to God. We might as well declare unabashed universalism that everyone is saved whether or not they repent.

How can we talk of repentance and of reconciliation without first assuming there is some prior alienation or hostility between God and us? Parties who are not alienated from each other don't need to be reconciled or re-established in their relationship.

The Biblical concept of reconciliation assumes a condition of estrangement between God and us. Much is said in Scripture of our hostility toward God. We are described as being God's enemies by nature and in sinful rebellion against Him.

On the other hand the contemporary view is although we are estranged from God, He is not estranged from us; that God goes on loving us with an unconditional love, winking at our sin so to speak, while we, in our fallen nature, hate Him. The cross illustrates this to be untrue.

Christ was not sacrificed on the cross as God's offering to us. His sacrifice was not to satisfy our unjust enmity toward God but to satisfy God's wrath toward our sin. It is to the Father, and not to Satan, to whom the Son's payment is made. The effect of the cross is to remove God's estrangement from us, not our estrangement from Him. While we were yet sinners, God loved us so much that He sent His only Son to die for us.

The cross occurred as a "condition" of God love for us. His love stands behind His plan of salvation. It is in the cross of Christ that the obstacle of our estrangement is overcome and we are reconciled to God. Remember His words of assurance in John 15:16 that we have not chosen Christ but that He, in His great love for us, has chosen us.

Alas and did my Savior bleed
And did my Sovereign die,
Would he devote that sacred head
For such a worm as I?
Was it for sins that I had done
He groaned upon the tree
Amazing pity, grace unknown
And love beyond degree
My God why would
You shed Your blood,
So pure and undefiled?
To make a sinful one like me,
Your chosen precious child.

What does *Sola Scriptura* mean?

It is a common misunderstanding that Protestants believe in the infallible authority of Scripture while Roman Catholics believe only in the infallibility of the Roman Catholic Church and her traditions. This is a distortion. Protestants and Roman Catholics alike acknowledge the infallible authority of the Bible. Where we differ is whether the Bible is the only infallible source of special revelation. Roman Catholics have held to two sources of infallible special revelation, Scripture and tradition.

Yet Protestants too have held to two kinds of revelation, general and special. General or natural revelation refers to

God's revelation of Himself in nature. Special revelation refers to the fact that there is but one written source of revelation, the Bible. This then is the "*sola*" of *sola Scriptura*. But Protestants also hold to traditional creeds, confessions and pronouncements that are the works of men. The chief reason then for "*sola*" is the conviction that the Bible alone is inspired by God, while creeds, confessions, etc. as accurate and brilliantly conceived as they may be by the best insights of learned scholars, are not the (direct) inspired Word of God.

So the question of *sola Scriptura* is one of authority in which the supreme authority rests with the Bible and not the church, with God and not with man. For Protestants it's a matter of subordinating the church and its traditions to the Bible and not the Bible to the church. The church gets its authority from the Bible; the Bible does not owe its authority to the church. Similarly our creeds and confessions have authority and validity from biblical teaching, they do not create the Bible's authority.

But somewhere many evangelical Protestants have become confused and have re-interpreted *sola Scriptura* (Scripture alone as a basis for the church, tradition, etc.) to now mean, only Scripture. Oftentimes Christians do not understand the doctrinal distinctions that separate evangelicalism from the plethora of movements that have trampled across the stage of Christendom. Many would describe God's triune nature in modalistic terms that deny the Trinity. Others hold a faulty view of *sola fide* (faith alone) and *sola gratia* (grace alone) that leads to antinomianism, while others swing to the other side and end up entangled in legalism. Likewise, the doctrine of *sola Scriptura* is not immune to misconceptions and distortion leading to what may be called only Scripture.

Only Scripture is an erroneous doctrine of Scripture that is based upon Anabaptist individualism, Enlightenment rationalism, and democratic populism. It is a doctrine of

Scripture divorced form its Christian context. It is no different than the doctrine of Scripture and tradition advocated by the Jehovah's Witnesses in numerous publications such as *Should You Believe in the Trinity?* in which individuals are urged to reject the ecumenical Christian creeds in favor of a new hermeneutical context.

"Sola" Scriptura is the doctrine wherein Scripture is the sole source of revelation, the perfect, sufficient, and final authoritative norm, inspired, and infallible. In sola Scriptura we have the proper relationship of Scripture, Church, and tradition. Scripture must be confessed as the sole source of revelation; it must be confessed as the only infallible, final and authoritative norm of doctrine and practice; it is to be interpreted in and by the Church; and it is to be interpreted according to the *regula fidei* (rule of faith).

If in holding to your "sovereignty of God," you believe God works all things according to the counsel of His will and that His knowledge of all things past, present, and future is infallible, then what is the point of praying that anything happen? If God has predestined some to be chosen before the foundation of the world, then what's the point in praying for anyone's conversion from unbelief?

The implicit argument in your question is that if prayer is to be possible humans must have the power of self-determination. That is, all human decisions must ultimately belong to mankind, not God. Otherwise human decisions are really fixed in God's eternal counsel.

Let's examine the biblical reasonableness of this. Scriptures is clear in that a person in need of conversion is "dead in trespasses and sins" (Ephesians 2:1); he is "enslaved to sin" (Romans 6:17; John 8:34); "the god of this world has blinded his mind that he might not see the light of the gospel of the glory of Christ" (II Corinthians. 4:4); his heart is hardened against God (Ephesians 4:18) so that he is hostile to God and in rebellion against God's will (Romans 8:7).

God cannot save humans unless God acts so as to change the human heart from hard hostility to tender trust. If you pray that God enlighten the mind of human beings so that they truly believe, you are in effect asking that God no longer to leave the determination of human will in our own power. You are asking God to do something within the human mind (or heart) so that we will surely see and believe. That is, you are conceding that the ultimate determination of human decision to believe is God's.

It is not the doctrine of God's sovereignty, which thwarts prayer for the conversion of sinners. On the contrary, it is the unbiblical notion of self-determination, which would consistently put an end to all prayers for the lost. Prayer is a request that God do something. But the only thing God can do to save a lost sinner is to overcome a person's resistance to God. If you insist that humans retain their self-determination, then you are insisting that humans remain in unbelief. John 6:44 tells us that no one can believe unless it is given him from the Father. Only the person who rejects human self-determination can consistently pray for God to save the lost. It was God alone who opened Lydia's heart so that she gave heed to what Paul said (Acts 16:14).

O.K., granted that a person's conversion is ultimately determined by God I still don't see the point of prayer. If God chose before the foundation of the world who would be converted, what function does prayer have?

Prayer has a function like that of preaching; "how shall the lost believe in whom they have not heard, and how shall they hear without a preacher, and how shall they preach unless they are sent (Romans 10:14f.)?" Belief is a gift of God (John 6:65; II Timothy 2:25; Ephesians 2:8), but God has ordained that the means by which a person believes is through the preaching of men.

It is simply naive to say that if no one spread the gospel all those predestined to be sons of God (Ephesians 1:5) would be converted anyway. The reason this is naive is because it overlooks the fact that the preaching of the gospel is just as predestined, as is the believing of the gospel. Paul was set apart for his preaching ministry before he was born (Galatians 1:15), as was Jeremiah (Jeremiah 1:5). Therefore, to ask, "If we don't evangelize, will the elect be saved?" is like asking, "If there is no predestination, will the predestined be saved?" God knows those who are His and He will raise up messengers to win them.

Prayer is like preaching in that it is also a human act. It is a human act that God has ordained in which He delights because it reflects the dependence of His creatures upon Him. He has promised to respond to prayer, and His response is just as contingent upon our prayer as our prayer is in accordance with his will. "And this is the confidence which we have before Him, that if we ask anything according to His will, He hears us" (I John 5:14).

In other words, just as God will see to it that His Word is proclaimed as a means to saving the elect, so He will see to it that all those prayers are prayed to which He has promised to respond. If God ordains the ends He surely ordains the means to those ends. Even our prayers are a gift from the One who "works in us that which is pleasing in his sight" (Hebrews 13:21).

Some friends of mine have stated that the doctrine of the Trinity is not biblical, are they correct?

The doctrine of the Trinity is not biblical in the sense that justification (Rom. 4, Gal. 2) or the doctrine of Christ (Col. 1, Phil. 2) is biblical. Also, it is not supported by specific "Trinitarian" passages. Rather, the doctrine of the Trinity is the result of considering how Scripture speaks of Father, Son, and Holy Spirit. Thus, the doctrine is forced on us to account for the unity-diversity of the three persons.

In the definition of Trinity there are three points: 1. there is but one God, 2. the Father, Son, and Holy Spirit is each a distinct person, 3. the Father, Son, and Holy Spirit is each God. (Perhaps the term Tri-unity would better account for both unity and diversity, but we are historically stuck with Trinity as a fixed term.) In this Tri-unity (or Trinity) both the oneness and the three-ness are equally ultimate, yet there is a priority of oneness over three-ness in terms of the order of revelation, but not in terms of ontology, that is, in nature of being.

This equal ultimacy removes any basis for "subordination" in regards to essence or being, but not in regards to persons. The Son and Holy Spirit, as God, are not generated, nor do they proceed in any fashion from the Father; in terms of substance they are equally ultimate as the Father. However, as persons they are indeed subordinate to the Father. The Father sends the Son, and the Father and the Son send the Holy Spirit.

While the Bible does not provide a well-rounded doctrine of the Trinity there are many allusions to it in Scripture. Here are a few:

- *Elohim* is a plural name for God, the Shema (Deut. 6:4) says the Lord is one but the word in Hebrew that is translated as one is *echad* (which means one in plurality) and it is the same word used in Genesis 2:24 where God says man shall cleave unto his wife and they shall be one *echad* (again one in plurality);
- In creation, God speaks of Himself in plurality (*Elohim*) and when He says "let *US*" (Gen. 1:26);
- We have the Threefold benediction in Num. 6:24-26 and in II Cor. 13:14;

- The Trisagion (Holy, Holy, Holy) in Isa. 6:3-6,
- God addressing Himself in Psa. 45:6,7 and Heb. 1:8,9;
- The outline of the Trinity in Isa. 63:7-14;
- In the Great Commission in Matt. 28:19 the command is to baptize in one name followed by an elliptical clause indicating that one name is the name of each person of the Trinity.

If Jesus is an equal person in the Trinity why does He say, as He does in John 14:28) that "the Father is greater than I"?

Indeed a critical question does arise where Jesus says that the Father is greater than He is (John 14:28) because it appears on surface to discredit the doctrine of the Trinity. This is why the church has always confessed a doctrine called the subordination of Christ (notice it is not called the inferiority of Christ).

Subordination does not necessarily imply inferiority. This is why in the Trinity we have a distinction among the persons of the Godhead. In the economy (plan) of redemption and even of creation we see certain works attributed to the Father, others to the Son and others to the Holy Spirit. The Son is subordinate to the Father in the work of redemption (thus He prayed to the Father) and the Holy Spirit is subordinate to both the Father and the Son. But that does not mean inequality of being or dignity or divine attributes, as all three persons are fully God in essence.

Christ is also called God in the New Testament in John 1:1,18; John 20:28; Romans 9:5; Titus 2:13; Hebrews 1:8; I John 5:30; (and in the Old Testament in Isaiah 9:6); yet is distinct from the Father in Psalm 2:7; Matthew 27:46; and John 5:32,37. Moreover, we read in Colosians 2:9, *For in him dwelleth all the fulness of the Godhead bodily*, the significant "*I AM*" statements in John (especially John 8:58

"*Before Abraham was, I AM,*" and John 10:30 "*I and my Father are one*"); He performed miracles; His birth was supernatural; He rose from the dead; He said He was the very manifestation of the Father in John 14:9; Jesus was the Creator of all "*All things were made by him; and without him was not any thing made that was made*" as we read in John 1:3, and He accepted worship of Himself.

Were Jesus not God He could not be our redeemer since biblically no man can redeem another with God. But, perhaps the most ringing endorsement of all is where God refers to Jesus as Son and as God in Hebres 1:8, "*But unto the Son He (God) says, Thy throne, O God, is forever and ever;*" the Father clearly calls the Son "God" in this verse.

In summary, in the Trinity while we have equal ultimacy or unity in that the Father is God, the Son is God, and the Holy Spirit is God; we also have diversity or distinctiveness of the three-ness in that the Son is not the Father, the Father is not the Holy Spirit, and the Holy Spirit is not the Son. Anything less results in super-subordinationism or monarchianism.

Recognizing that the orthodox Trinitarian position has its limitations due to human thought and language in describing the ineffable mystery of "three in oneness" the Trinity remains as the only view that sets forth the Father, Son and Holy Spirit as co-equal and co-eternal in the Godhead with regard to both divine essence and function.

Does the robe my pastor wears mean something? Is it biblical?

When the church on earth gathers on the Lord Day she enters into heaven (by faith) to worship God with the all of the angelic host and the departed saints. It is as if the roof of our church building is torn off when the pastor calls the people to worship. Worshipers enter and are all organized around the throne of God. The worship service does not merely provide an opportunity for private devotional experiences. The church is a "city" and a "joyous assembly" or "festal array" (Hebrews 12:22-24).

In Christian worship, biblically and historically, pastors wear distinctive garments to testify to their office as representatives of Christ. The robe serves to hide the personality of an individual and highlight one's special calling. The pastor represents Christ, the Husband, to the church, His bride. When the pastor leads worship, the robe helps remind us that it is not "my friend Joe" up front. God in Christ calls us to worship, to confess, to hear His word, to give, etc., and He does so by means of His called servant. The pastor does not act as an individual, but for Christ.

Judges, police officers and others wear a uniform because they do not act for themselves; they are under orders. They represent the law and government of the county, city, or state in which they serve. In the same way, a pastor represents the law and government of another kingdom. The clothing a pastor wears testifies to this. A pastor is also under orders. The pastor does not derive authority from economic or social status, or by looking and acting like other leaders in the world in business suits, even though this is what happens too often in America. Just as the location of the pulpit and table have symbolic significance, so also the pastor's clothing communicates that the pastor is the servant of the risen Christ, called to lead God's people in covenant renewal worship.

In the Bible clothing and calling are often connected; a person's calling or office together with whatever authority is connected with the office is often visually symbolized by the clothing the person wears (Genises 9:20-27; 39:1-13; 37: 3-11, 23; 41:1-44; all of the references in Exodus and Leviticus to the clothing of the priests; 1 Samuel 2:19; 15:27; 18:4; 24:4, 5, 11, 14; Ezra 9:3-5; Esther 8:15; Isaiah 22:21; Jonah 3:6; Matthew 22:11ff.; 27:31; Mark 16:5; Luke 15:22; and Revelation 1:13; 4:4; 6:11; 19:13, 16). The purpose of the robe is to cover a person and accent one's calling by God.

Therefore, by wearing a robe a pastor is seeking to bring a practice in line with what the Bible implies, back in line with what the historic Church has practiced, and in line with what many other churches continue to do worldwide.

What are the various end times or eschatological views?

Eschatology is a twenty-dollar word that comes from the Greek and literally means last discourse. It is the doctrine of last things and end times covering all of creation. It is related to the second coming of Christ (often referred to as the time of the Rapture) and millenarianism or chiliasm. The second coming of Christ is also referred to in theology as the parousia, from the Greek word meaning coming or presence.

Millenarianism or chiliasm are two additional twenty-dollar words that mean the same thing, a belief in a 1,000 year period at the end of the age when Christ shall come again. Bookstores, especially Christian bookstores, have shelves filled with literature about the end times. Most recent has been the Left Behind series.

Millennialists are divided into three general views. Those who expect that the Lord will return before the millennium (the 1,000 year period at the end of the present age when Jesus Christ reigns with his people over the earth) are called Premillennialists. Those who hold that the second coming will take place after the millennium (a golden age on earth in which the church is triumphant) are called Postmillennialists. The third view holds that there is no sufficient Scriptural ground for the expectation of a millennium. There will be no literal 1,000 year reign of Christ on earth but His second coming on the last day will usher in eternal paradise for some and eternal damnation for others. Those who hold to this third view are know as Amillennialists.

Premillennialists may be divided into three sub-groups. The first sub-group is known as Historic Premillennialists and says that Jesus will come back for His own one thousand years before the end of the world. The other two sub groups are classified as Dispensational Premillennialists. One group says that Jesus will come back for His own one thousand and seven years before the end of the world. A second group says that He will come back for His own one thousand three and a half years before the end of the world.

Preterism is an eschatological view that places most or all last times events in the past, especially during the destruction of Jerusalem in 70 A. D. Its views range from placing all of the end times events in the first century to most of those end times events with the exception of the Second Coming, and the final judgment.

In your biography, I noticed your affinity for the New York Yankees. Since the Bible does start with words about the *"beg-inning"* may I ask what team was the greatest Yankee team?

I pray the questioner enjoys reminiscing about Yankee history as much as I do. I can remember the thrill of attending my first Yankee game at the age of nine in 1947. Taking the bus from College Point to Flushing. Walking down several flights of stairs to the Flushing, Main Street Station where we, my parents and I, boarded the subway. Within a minute the train emerged from underground onto the elevated tracks and traveled east until it reached the East River. The train went underground again and we disembarked at Grand Central Station where we went up several steep escalators to the Lexington Line and boarded the Woodlawn-Jerome subway. We made our way to the first car where I stood enthralled as the dimly lit tracks and pillars rushed toward me until finally the train emerged from the darkness onto the elevated tracks, the majestic Yankee Stadium suddenly appearing bigger than life beside the station at 161st. Street.

Once in the ballpark, I saw for the first time, in their traditional pinstripe livery, the greatest team in baseball, THE NEW

YORK YANKEES. Now those '47 Yankees were an excellent team, but certainly not the greatest of all Yankee teams. There was number 5, the "Yankee Clipper", Joe DiMaggio, number 15, "Old Reliable" Tommy Henrich, number 6, "Doctor" Bobby Brown and number 22, the "Super Chief" Allie Reynolds among others like Phil Rizzuto, "Yogi" Berra, George McQuinn, George "Snuffy" Stirnweiss and Johnny Lindell. That Yankee team won the pennant by 12 games, winning a total of 97 plus four as they defeated the archenemy, the Brooklyn Dodgers in a seven game World Series.

I looked up to and emulated these athletes when I was a boy, and nothing I have discovered has or ever will change my attitude toward them. It is one thing that has enriched my life and allowed me to transcend the realities of everyday life. Over the next 18 years, the Yankees rewarded my allegiance with 15 American League pennants, losing only in 1948 and (despite winning 103 games) in 1954 to the Cleveland Indians, and then in 1959 to the Chicago White Sox. During those 15 Fall Classic appearances from 1947 through 1964, the Yankees won 10 World Series Championships. It was difficult for me not to assume that God was a Yankee fan.

Perhaps the greatest advantage of being a Yankee fan and growing up in NYC during that era was that I had the ability to "see" every game on radio. The "Voice of the Yankees," Mel Allen could describe the details of each pitch and play so vividly, that my mind's eye gave me a choice seat behind home plate for every game, home or away. I literally "saw" better ball games on radio, due to Mel's play by play announcing than any game seen on television. Mel also taught his millions of listeners and me everything one needs to know to appreciate the game. To this day I can recite the "Infield Fly Rule" verbatim, because I heard Mel Allen state it over and over whenever an umpire would call one.

The Yankees have dominated the game of baseball from the glory of "Babe" Ruth and the "Iron Man" Lou Gehrig, to the grace of Joe DiMaggio, to the reign of Mickey Mantle and Casey Stengel, through the turmoil of Reggie Jackson, Thurman Munson and Billy Martin, to the 1998 World Champion team with their 125 total victories and into the twenty-first century teams of Jeter and A-Rod. For the current team the word money is a double entendre. Admittedly, they are the money players in the finest tradition of athletes who produce under pressure, yet the Yankees rule baseball as no other major team ever has.

Some have said that the 1998 team was the greatest Yankee team of all time. But were they really the best major league team of all time as an article in the October 16, 1998 issue of The Wall Street Journal concluded? Indeed it was true that the 1998 team could only compete with the great teams of the past but I contend that the WSJ article consisted of inappropriate comparisons that led to false conclusions.

The authors of that article, Barra and Meyer, only compared the 1998 Yankee team to the 1927 Yankee team and erroneously concluded that only Ruth and Gehrig could break into the 1998 team's starting line-up. In their comparison, they over looked several other great Yankee teams of the past who may make equal claim. Consider the 1961 Yankee team of Mantle and Maris. In comparing the 1961 team with the 1998 team, Mantle and Maris would certainly replace Williams and O'Neill in center and right field. In comparing the 1961 versus 1998 infields I would take Richardson for his fielding over Knoblaugh; Howard, who batted .348 with 21 home runs would win out as catcher over Posada who hit .268 with 17 home runs; and Berra and Blanchard (sharing left field) would win out over the 1998 left field trio of Spencer, Ledee, and Raines. In 1961, Whitey Ford, at 25 and 4 with a 3.21 ERA, and reliever Luis Arroyo with his 2.19 ERA would surely earn spots on the 1998 team. Thus, the 1961 Yankees matched up well with the 1998 team.

The WSJ authors also ignored the great Yankee teams of the late 1930's. From 1936 through 1939 they won four pennants and four World Series. In four years they won 409 regular season games plus twelve World Series games while losing only three. The 1938 and 1939 teams swept the best the National League could offer, the Cubs and Reds respectively. I would think DiMaggio, Gehrig, Dickey, Selkirk, Keller and Gordon might have earned spots on the 1998 roster despite Barra and Meyer ignoring their accomplishments. Red Ruffing and Lefty Gomez could have earned a turn or two on the mound for the 1998 team.

Going back to the 1927 team, the authors Barra and Meyer erred in major regards when they rejected Tony "Push 'em up" Lazzeri , "Long Bob" Meusel and "Colonel" Earle Combs on the basis of their life time averages. In 1998, Scott Brosius wins out at third base, but only if one considers the lifetime performances of other Yankee "hot corner" specialists like "Jumppin" Joe Dugan, Red Rolfe, Clete Boyer or Gil McDougald? Even if one views Lazzeri's 1927 stats only (.309 BA with 18 round 'trippers), Tony would be my choice over Knoblauch. Barra and Neyer select Bernie Williams because Meusel hit "just .309 for his career" ignoring the fact that he hit .337 in 1927. Combs was eliminated because "he hit .325 in twelve seasons." I would again refer Barra and Meyer to Combs' stats of 1927 when he hit .356, 36 doubles and led the league with 23 triples and question whether Paul O'Neill would, as they put it, "eat Mr. Combs's lunch and steal his dessert."

Barra and Meyer further revealed their lack of knowledge of Yankee history when they made the following inappropriate comparisons. In 1927, Combs was the center fielder, Meusel the left fielder and Ruth was in right. Therefore Messers. Barra and Neyer, should have compared Combs with Williams and not with O'Neill; Meusel with the 1998 left field trio; and Ruth, not Combs, with O'Neill. Then all three '27 outfielder's, based on their performances in that year, would replace the 1998 Yankee outfield. I also would not dismiss the '27 Yankee pitching staff as swiftly as these authors did. The '27 staff boasted a combined 3.20 ERA, led by Wilcy Moore's 2.28, Waite Hoyt's 2.64, Urban Schocker's 2.84, and Herb Pennock's 3.00.

The authors Barra and Meyer were right in that there is no current or past team in either league that could compete with the 1998 Yankee team. Those 1998 Yankees were a great team, but NOT alone the greatest of all. That title belongs generically to all the great Yankee teams, past and present. From any viewpoint, the Yankees are baseball's greatest team. They are today and they always have been. That is their reputation and that is their tradition. Its great to be a Yankee fan! Hey Mel Allen, "How about that?"

I also noticed you went to a Yankee Fantasy Camp. What was the most inspiring memory that you have from that week?

Obviously I have many good memories from that week in which we played two games a day "with our heroes in pinstripes" of the past. At the particular camp I attended, the 1961 infield of Bill "Moose" Skowron, Bobby Richardson, Tony Kubek and Clete Boyer was featured.

One of my earliest recollections of that week was when I put on the Yankee uniform for the first time and walked by a mirror in the locker room. While I am not implying any sacredness to the Yankee livery, I realized that the momentary joy I experienced was but a mere finite shadow of the infinite joy I will have when one day I stand clothed in the righteous of Christ.

It was a thrill to play and meet with one of my all-time Yankee favorites Bobby Richardson. Between games each day we would eat in the locker room where I was honored when another of all-time Yankee favorite of mine, shortstop and later NBC announcer Tony Kubek, would sit with me to discuss theological issues.

Each night we would all gather around and toss questions at these Yankee legends. One evening someone asked Don Mattingly if he thought he had "retired one year to early?" Mattingly was one of the greatest first basemen in Yankee history having played for them from late 1982 through his retirement year of 1995; years in which the Yankees did not play in the World Series. The year following Mattingly's retirement the Yankees won it all, thus the reason for the question being asked of him.

Mattingly, who at that time had hair down to his shoulders and sported a Fu-Manchu moustache, did not answer immediately. Then he gave an answer that I'll never forget. Mattingly said, " No," paused, and then added, "I never look back and ask why, but rather I always look up and give thanks." All of the world's greatest sermons have never said so much in so few words. As I complete my writing of this book and you the reading of it, let us both remember to always look up and give thanks. Soli Deo Gloria!

Printed in the United States
46897LVS00003B/1-123

9 781597 818940